A Faith That Remains

A Faith That Remains

Kenneth M. Blackwell

Fealty Publishing
Bemidji, Minnesota.

A Faith That Remains.

By Kenneth M. Blackwell

Published by:
Fealty Publishing,
Post Office Box 1071,
Bemidji, Minnesota 56619-1071
www.fealtypublishing.com

All rights reserved. No part of this book may be reproduced except for the inclusion of brief quotations in a review.

Copyright © 2003 by Kenneth M. Blackwell.

"Scripture quotations taken from the New American Standard Bible ®, Copyright © 1960,1962,1963, 1968,1971,1972,1973, 1975,1977,1995 by the Lockman Foundation. Used by permission." (http://www.Lockman.org)

Cover Design: Studio Arts - www.studioartsonline.com

ISBN, print edition: 0-9727303-0-3

Printed in the United States of America.

Library of Congress Control Number: 2002096052

*Dedicated to my wife Jan,
who shares the journey.
And my sons, Daniel, Stephen, Andrew and Peter.
May they too know the joy of following hard after God.*

CONTENTS

Introduction	Apprehended by God	*13*
Chapter one	A Passion for Ministry	*17*
Chapter two	Hearing God	*27*
Chapter three	Taking Ourselves Seriously	*39*
Chapter four	Men of Faith Don't Whine	*51*
Chapter five	Poolside and Rooftop	*63*
Chapter six	Faith Involves Risk	*79*
Chapter seven	Increase Our Faith	*95*
Chapter eight	Looking Up To Heaven	*103*
Chapter nine	It Takes Guts to Say "Jesus"	*111*
Chapter ten	The Righteous Live by Their Faith	*123*
Chapter eleven	Audacious Faith	*135*
Chapter twelve	From Tragedy to Triumph	*147*
Chapter thirteen	So What	*155*
Chapter fourteen	Destination Unknown	*169*
Chapter fifteen	Endurance	*177*

"One of the saddest feelings in the world is the feeling that your life is going nowhere. You're alive. But you feel that there is no point in being alive. You get a little daydream—a little flicker—of what it might be like to be a part of something really great and really valuable, and what it might be like to have a significant part in it. But then you wake up and everything looks so small and insignificant and pitiful and out of the way and unknown and pointless.

We were not made to live without a destiny. We were made to be sustained by a meaningful, purposeful future. We were made to be strengthened each day by this assurance, this confidence, that what is happening in our lives today, no matter how mundane and ordinary is a really significant step toward something great and good and beautiful tomorrow."

John Piper, "God's Invincible Purpose, Part Two: Foundations for Full Assurance" (sermons delivered at Bethlehem Baptist Church, Minneapolis, MN, 8 March 1992) [on-line]; available from http://desiringgod.org; Internet. Used by permission.

"It is very easy to think that the great days of religion are past. It is told that a child, on being told some of the great old testament stories, said wistfully: "God was much more exciting then." There is a continual tendency in the church to look back, to believe that God's power is grown less and that the golden days lay behind. The writer to Hebrews sounds forth a trumpet call. 'Never think,' he says, that you have arrived too late in history; never think that the days of great promise and great achievement lie behind.' This is still God's 'today'. There is a blessedness for you as great as the blessedness of the saints; there is an adventure for you as great as the adventure of the martyrs. God is as great today as ever He was."

William Barclay, THE LETTER TO THE HEBREWS (Daily Study Bible Series), published by Westminster John Knox Press. Used by permission.

Apprehended by God

introduction

Who me?

Out of the blue the thought popped into my head, "Why don't you apply?" The youth program in our church which my wife Jan and I headed up had grown to the point where it was felt the services of a full time youth pastor were necessary. I enjoyed working with the kids but had no aspiration to work full time for the church as a youth pastor. I dismissed the thought immediately but it came back the next day. I rejected it again. But I couldn't get it out of my mind and started coming home from work early each day where I would just sit and reflect on this novel and incredible idea. "Put my name forward to be a youth pastor? Ah that is silly," I told myself . I had my own plans and they didn't include being a youth pastor.

But the thought would not go away. For over a week I pondered the matter without saying anything to anyone. At the end of the second week I told Jan. Then I sought the counsel of a minister friend to ask if he thought I was hearing from God. He told me his own personal experience was that if something did not go away that was usually a good sign it was from God. God wanted me! To be a youth pastor! That was a little bit too fantastic to take in. "Ok Lord, if you want me to be the youth pastor I will do it," I prayed. Immediately the burden was lifted.

That was the beginning of everything. Although I applied for the position of youth pastor I was not selected. It was just the opportunity God used to ask me if I would be willing to lay down my own ambitions and make myself available for His purposes. This encounter with God changed the course of my life and since then my whole orientation has been to live out God's will for my life.

Paul the Apostle said, "For you have died and your life is hidden with Christ in God" (Colossians 3:3). The paradox, though, is that death to my own self interest has been life in all its fullness. God has taken Jan and me overseas to places we never imagined we would ever go: Africa, Europe, the middle East, and to America twice. We left our native New Zealand in 1988 and have made our home in Northern Minnesota these years since. God's purposes for our life have gone far beyond anything we could ever have imagined. When God led me to America, I went with nothing more to go on than God's word that it was for a time of learning and preparation. There I discovered writing. One cold January morning walking to the trailer that served as a classroom at a Bible school in Northern Minnesota, I fell in step with the teacher who had in his hand the writing assignments he had given us students. He handed me mine with the comment, "If this is your writing, then Christian writing or journalism may be your calling." That was new, and he was right. Shortly afterward we went to Israel and Europe and on the trip I began to take notes. I have not stopped taking notes since. I keep a pad handy to jot down observations. If I go somewhere I stop and make notes as a thought comes into my head. In church, listening to the preacher, I make notes. As I read or watch TV I make notes. Looking around my office I can see notes, hundreds of notes. They are the raw material from which I write.

"You are a communicator. God's going to cause knowledge to flow through you," was a word of knowledge spoken over me by a minister after I came back to New Zealand from America. I believe the Holy Spirit confirmed my calling. Subsequently I have preached God's word and taught Sunday school classes. I have written a Christian column in a newspaper communicating the gospel to a secular audience. Now I am writing this book which I hope will inspire readers to make it an imperative to discover God's will for their lives. It is no happy accident of fate that when we dedicate ourselves to uncovering His will for our life we will find the niche we are to fill in this world.

Speaking to the prophet Jeremiah God said, "Before I formed you in the womb I knew you, And before you were born I consecrated you; I have appointed you a prophet to the nations" (Jeremiah 1:5). We were created for a purpose. When we fulfill the role God has prepared for us we find our identity. To uncover our God-given gifts and talents is to discover what makes us unique; to function in those same talents gives purpose and meaning to our life. I thank God for calling me to do what I want to do anyway. I love to write. I love to study God's word. Serving God is not one more burden to be borne on shoulders already heavy laden. God's work is a good busyness. I can easily spend all day making notes, carefully selecting and arranging them to craft a piece of writing that communicates God's word to others. Away from my office I am writing in my head. Any prolonged length of time away from my study and I am eager to be back writing. And that is remarkable, for growing up I never had a talent or even an interest in writing. This has been God's gift, a supernatural gift of the Spirit to fill the calling He has placed on my life, and it is wonderful in my eyes.

When Nathaniel first met Jesus He was greeted with the remark, "Behold, an Israelite indeed, in whom is no guile!" Taken aback, Nathanael replied "How do You know me?" Jesus answered and said to him, "Before Philip called you, when you were under the fig tree, I saw you." Observing his awestruck reaction Jesus commented, "You are impressed because I told you about yourself, you shall see greater things than this." Jesus knows us intimately. Our private thoughts, the longings of our heart, are no secret to Him. He knows our struggles, He knows every twist and turn we have taken in the road. When we meet Him we find out how well He knows us, and how ready He is to receive us and link His life with ours, in an adventure that goes beyond anything we had ever envisaged.

...but just as it is written, 'things which eye has not seen and ear has not heard, and which have not entered the heart of man, all that God has prepared for those who love Him

(1 Corinthians 2:9).

A Passion for Ministry

chapter one

Toward the end of the 1996 Presidential elections, in a last ditch effort to rescue his flagging campaign, Republican candidate Bob Dole attacked the Democrats over some dubious campaign contributions. "Where is the outrage, America?" he repeated in rallies across the country. Dole knew what it would take to get votes: find an issue that would arouse people's passions. He got no argument from the Democrats about the need to reform campaign contributions; politicians in both parties agreed something ought to be done to prevent the so called "soft money" contributions of big investors from influencing and buying political favors.

It is history that Dole did not win the election. The issue raised no little indignation among the voting public, but the feelings were not strong enough to carry an election. I wrote an article in the post election period in which I wondered if the actions of either political party over this issue would match their rhetoric. "Without the ire of an angry public to prod them," I wrote, "there is every likelihood that any reform bill eventually passed may be so watered down as to render it ineffectual."

I was right. Three years later, December 1999, in the first primary of the 2000 presidential elections, came this news report out of Claremont, New Hampshire: "Portraying themselves as political outsiders, Democrat Bill Bradley and Republican John McCain pledged to pursue genuine campaign finance reform in a rare bipartisan appearance ... on the same site that in 1995 President Clinton and then house speaker Newt Gingrich had pledged to form a commission to reform campaign laws. That panel never materialized!" Without the outrage a just cause was shelved until another election gave it new life.

My subject is passion. Where is the passion in the church for ministry? Christians regularly pray for revival and profess a longing to see godless people accept Christ as their Savior. I sometimes wonder if there is a deep concern for the unsaved or whether the church is merely going through the motions when it gets involved in the work of God. We do it because we know we ought to, but our heart isn't really in it. I took part in an evangelism outreach into the community. The turnout of volunteers from area churches for the pre-outreach meeting was impressive. However, the post rally meeting four weeks later drew only about fifteen percent of those who had started out in a gush of enthusiasm. If that is an indication of the enthusiasm there is in the church, can we really expect God to answer prayers for revival? As Christians we bemoan the way the world is going - the broken marriages, the lack of virtue, increasing violence. Yes, we want revival, but we get cranky when church goes twenty minutes late. For all our talk about revival how much ardor lies behind the rhetoric?

Some Christians think it is unspiritual to be passionate about anything. They say, "Have faith, God will do it in His

A Passion For Ministry

own time. Just wait, be patient." These people have their spiritual cliches for the lack of converts, "God builds the church, we just spread the gospel. We plant the seed, God brings in the harvest in His season." But I want to pose a question: could it be that God is withholding revival because there is not a real passion in the church for revival? The statement is often made that the key to revival is prayer. But what kind of prayer? Is it the prayer of rote offered up in a prayer meeting by one whose attention is elsewhere? Is that prayer going to engage God's attention? Could it be that the prayers offered up in a monotone by a stone faced church member at a prayer meeting are about as inspiring to God as they are to the petitioner's contemporaries who are nodding off to sleep nearby?

There is a story related in the bible concerning the prophet Elisha and Joash the king of Israel. Reports came to Joash of Elisha's sickness and imminent death. Joash was very agitated at the news, for he recognized that Elisha, more than any other man in Israel, was responsible for the nation's success against the Syrian invaders who constantly warred against them. For over sixty years and six kings Elisha's prayers had petitioned God on behalf of the nation. Joash rushed to Elisha's bedside and here's how the Bible records that death bed scene:

> *Joash wept over Elisha saying, "My father, my father, the chariots of Israel and its horsemen!" And Elisha said to him, "Take a bow and arrows." So he took a bow and arrows.*
>
> *Then he said to the king of Israel, "Put your hand on the bow." And he put his hand on it, then Elisha laid his hands on the king's hands. And he said, "Open the window toward the east," and he opened it. Then Elisha said, "Shoot!" And he shot. And he*

said, "The Lord's arrow of victory, even the arrow of victory over Aram; for you shall defeat the Arameans at Aphek until you have destroyed them." Then he said, "Take the arrows," and he took them. And he said to the king of Israel, "Strike the ground," and he struck it three times and stopped. So the man of God was angry with him and said, "You should have struck five or six times, then you would have struck Aram until you would have destroyed it. But now you shall strike Aram only three times" (2Kings 13:12-19).

God was ready to give the king of Israel deliverance from the Syrian threat once and for all, but because the king lacked passion and was half-hearted in his response, Israel would only get a partial victory. The Syrians would remain as adversaries and continue to threaten Israel's borders. This story is a sobering reminder to us of the need to sustain our enthusiasm in spiritual matters. It is not all up to God. Our lack of enthusiasm may well lie behind the dearth of converts in the church.

I have observed over the years how the work of the church falls to a few. I have watched people put their names down to be involved and then not show up when the time comes to perform. They are simply too busy, perhaps something else comes up, or they just simply forget! Ministry has low appeal to the average church member. When revival comes we are going to see people delivered from their spiritual enemies. The power of debilitating sins which have haunted men and women all their lives is going to be broken. Proud men are going to humble themselves and ask God's forgiveness openly in public. Men are going to weep and ask their wives' forgiveness for years of physical abuse. Wives are going to ask forgiveness of their husbands for years of mental abuse. Young men and women living together are going to renounce that lifestyle and come before God to be married and seek His blessing on their union. Drug addicts are going to quit their habit, drunks are going to swear off the bottle. Hardened criminals are going to be ashamed of their behavior and beg for God's mercy. Nominal Christians are going to be on fire for God. All this and much more. As a Christian do you want to see this?

I must ask myself some pertinent questions when praying for revival. How much do I really want it? Am I prepared for services that go on for several hours, am I willing to find time for mid week prayer meetings? Attending the needs of so many new converts will be beyond the ability of a professional pastoral staff and inevitably more demands will be placed upon the congregation. Many of us are already overworked and overstressed. Staying up at all night prayer meetings and walking the streets witnessing takes time and energy we simply don't have ... unless a passion is kindled that lends wings to our leaden feet.

Where do we find that passion?

Toward the end of a life poured out in ministry the Apostle Paul declared "I press on to lay hold of that for which I was laid hold of." Now there is the passion for service God is looking for. In spite of setbacks - and there were many, enough to break the will of a lesser dedication - Paul's enthusiasm and energy in establishing churches through Asia never slackened. We all know the story of how Paul encountered the Lord on the road to Damascus. Blinded, he received his sight back only when Ananias laid hands on him. He was then baptized, filled with the Holy Spirit and immediately began to proclaim Jesus in the synagogues. Subsequently God revealed His will for Paul to reach the Gentiles with the gospel. Looking back Paul describes his experience as having been "laid hold of." Like Paul we need to be "laid hold of."

When we read the biography of any great man or woman of God, we see that somewhere there was a signal event that set them apart to do the work of God. Moses had his burning bush, Jacob wrestled with the angel, and Paul was blinded on the road to Damascus. In various and manifold ways since, God has always gotten the attention of men and women and set them apart to do His work. Before we too quickly dismiss the call of God as a peculiar distinction reserved for a select few within the church we should ask ourselves the question, "Why are we saved?" Is it no more than a ticket to heaven when we die? Scripture tells us *"we are His workmanship, created in Christ Jesus for good works, which God prepared beforehand, that we should walk in them" (Ephesians 2:10).* Our salvation is a call to ministry, just like Paul's. Wouldn't you think, dear saint, God would want to lay hold of you in the same way He did Paul?

He does! Your encounter with Christ may not be as dramatic as Paul's, but then again perhaps it will be. Whether it is sensational or not, it will be with the same life changing effect, a purpose driven faith that can say, like Paul, "I was laid hold of." The great tragedy in the church is that many do not really see ministry as a personal responsibility. Their feelings are summed up in the words, "leave it to the minister, that is what he is paid for." So far as these people are concerned the minister is the one who is "called," and they are simply there to support him, but there is no clergy - laity distinction with God. The commission to minister is given to all: *"But you are a chosen race, A royal priesthood, a holy nation, a people for God's own possession, that you may proclaim the excellencies of*

A Passion For Ministry

Him who has called you out of darkness into His marvelous light" (1 Peter 2:9). In these words the apostle Peter tells us it is the task of every believer to get out and proclaim the good news. Why then do so many believers lack a passion for ministry?

The trouble with many Christians whose whole experience is dry is that their religion has become inward. God's work is not something that occupies their thoughts because it does not hold their interest. They have lost their sense of the call of God to service. These people are not actively engaged in ministry as God intended, so their spiritual vitality is at a low ebb. In an attempt to put some zest back into their spiritual life they go off to conferences and meetings looking for renewal and refreshing, when the revival they need is a Pentecostal revival - a work of the Holy Spirit on their hearts that sets their affections upon ministry. Until ministry is personally desirable it can never be compelling. Jesus said His will was to do God's will. Only when the will of God becomes my will and satisfies a deep urge at the center of my being will I find the passion and fire for ministry that never dims.

When the resurrected Lord appeared to the disciples He instructed them to go out into all the world with the gospel. But first they must remain in Jerusalem and wait for what the Father had promised, *"Which,"* He said, *"you heard of from Me; for John baptized with water, but you shall be baptized with the Holy Spirit not many days from now"* (Acts 1:4, 5). The baptism in the Spirit was first and foremost an empowering for service. It is as necessary today as it was two thousand years ago; and available to contemporary Believers, just as it was to the early disciples. We need the Holy Spirit to come upon the church as tongues of fire, and if we confess our indifference to ministry and spiritual things, I believe He will.

"Oh Lord come and touch me with your Spirit. Lay your hand on me so that when I stand up I am not the same man. I confess I am indifferent to those things that matter most to you. Fill me Lord with your Spirit so that your will becomes my will. Amen."

Have you ever thought that God has a purpose for your life? Something more than showing up for church on Sunday and throwing a few bucks in the collection plate. As a fairly new Christian, not long saved, I taught a Sunday school class using lesson material I was given. One I remember was titled, 'God has a wonderful plan for your life.' I doubt I had ever thought in terms of God having a plan for my life. Had you asked me about my salvation I would have said it meant being saved from the wrath of God. I knew what I was saved from, but had no idea what I was saved for. Or even that there was a "what for."

But there is a "what for" and His plan for our life is truly unique. As singular as we are in personality and physical appearance from one another, so are God's intentions for our lives. When God formed us, he did so in the foreknowledge and after the counsel of His own will with regard to His plan for our lives. When we discover God's plan for our lives we will find ourselves doing what we were created for. That is why God's plan for us is so wonderful; it is personally fulfilling.

The purpose of this book is to lead you to ask yourself the question "Lord what is your will for my life?" It is quite simply the most significant question you can ever ask. If you have been in church and said to yourself, "God never speaks to me like others claim He speaks to them. I never really had a faith experience," then this question will change everything. It will take your spiritual experience out of the ho hum and make it a dynamic adventure in which Jesus' promise of life in all its fullness will become a reality. There is nothing more stimulating than being in sync with God's will. It will take you from the periphery of the church into the center of God's work. An arrow in God's hand that hits the mark!

The Apostle Paul was not an icon or aberration in the history of the church. Let me say that again in case you missed it. Paul was not some freak. He was a man called of God as you and I are. He was a man with the God-given task of taking the gospel into the world, the same work God has called you and me to do. Paul's ministry was his passion. The same passion and love for ministry can be ours. The only difference between us and Paul are the times in which we live and the ministry to which we are called. The apostle Paul had a special role to play in the history of the church, but then so do you and I. We too are writing the history of the church with our lives.

Now I am asking you, child of God, why don't you see what would happen if you set your mind to know the will of God for your life!

Hearing God

chapter two

Faith comes from hearing God.
You must hear God for yourself.

I once went to a meeting by an evangelist with a healing ministry. Afterward I was part of a group chatting with him and someone noted how the power of God had been there to heal during the service. He recalled that when he started out in ministry very few that he prayed for were healed; some people he said got worse instead of better. "As I was praying for people, medics and helpers were carrying out on stretchers the ones I had already prayed for. They came forward on a stretcher, they went out on a stretcher. That was humbling."

There are some hard lessons to be learned when we attempt to walk out God's will in our life, things can go wrong before they go right. When we were passed over as youth pastor we were left with a call of God on our life, but no idea what God wanted of us. At the time I was in debt from a previous business enterprise growing tomatoes and cucumbers in glasshouses. Jan and I concluded that perhaps we needed to pay this money back and get our affairs in order, then maybe God would show us. It was a lot of money, over a year's salary, but we paid it all back and right about the same time the house we rented was sold and we had to move. We thought the timing of this significant. Perhaps God was ready for us to move into His purposes. The only trouble was He still had not revealed what His will was.

Setting out to walk by faith is a little like learning to walk all over again. God's word says "My ways are higher than your ways"... "My thoughts are not like your thoughts." Elsewhere in the bible the apostle Paul tells us the wisdom of this world is foolishness to God and vice versa. These verses suggest that if we are to live our life by faith in God then the wisdom and logic by which we have ordered our life to this point are irrelevant, the rules have changed. So we did something that was totally foolish and impractical by all sound reasoning, but well, hopefully sensible and reasonable according to the measure God uses for wisdom. We gave up our jobs and waited for God to show us the next step. Since Jan's sister and her husband had offered us the use of their basement flat, we decided we would not look to find a new place or get a job or do anything until God revealed how we were to walk out His will in our life. Let's go all out, we agreed. We will put ourselves absolutely at God's mercy and trust Him. This was our response of faith. Oh we were such greenhorns, so naive, altogether lacking in both experience and discernment. But we were ever so enthusiastic and sincere, so eager to do the will of God. That's all that mattered - moving ahead into the purposes of God for our life. Whatever faith it took, we were determined to be up to it.

In those days I was enormously impressed by the testimonies of so many people like Corrie Ten Boom and

Hearing God 29

Brother Andrew who had given up their lives to serve God. I had read their stories of how they were used of God, and how He provided their needs, often with a miracle at the last minute. These people were my heroes, they were prepared to step out in faith. Well, by golly, Jan and I would too. Steadily our money dwindled, but there was no word from God. This was just a test. He was taking us to the edge to check out how strong our faith was. We were not going to back down, we would show God we had faith. With our brand new "go for broke faith" we waited for God to reveal the next stage in His purpose for our lives. Slowly the money ran out and finally the day came when we used the last to pay our rent. We had some gas in the car - when that ran out or we had to pay next weeks rent, whichever came first, that would be it. God had to show us before then. So, Ok, God was testing us a little more than we had anticipated. It was really getting down to the wire, but God always comes through at the last minute. After all, that is how God works. At least that seemed to be how it was with other faith heroes whose stories I had read, and I didn't intend to quit at the last minute. But God doesn't always go by the book, as I was to learn. The gas gauge was getting toward empty. I stuck some chewing gum over it. I didn't want to see how low it was getting because it might shake my faith. I reminded myself of Corrie Ten Boom's story of the concentration camp and her bottle of ointment that never ran out. I knew how faith worked. We are going to have one heck of a miracle here, a real beauty, how we drove 500 miles on a gallon of gas. Move over Corrie Ten Boom! Then it happened. The car gave a couple of surges and stopped. Just like that we ran out of gas, and there I was sitting holding the steering wheel in the car of faith that ran out of gas.

Our car ran out of gas and with it our brand new go for broke faith. God had not provided the direction we sought, which was after all the object of our faith. Did this mean the Lord had not called us as we believed? Had we got it all wrong about serving him? We were both pretty shaken and confused. Good friends Tony and Denny prevailed upon us to give it one more shot, which is how we ended up staying in a mobile trailer parked in their back yard. "One more week" they said, "give it one more week with us. We will pray with you and see if God will show His will for you." We agreed. What was one more week? If nothing else it would give us time to sort ourselves out. We were pretty low.

Each morning Tony and Denny counseled us and prayed with us for the direction we sought from God. As the days went by, Jan and I prayed and we read the Bible looking for answers. We talked until there was nothing left to say. But no word of direction from God. Every morning we met with Tony and Denny for counsel they would ask us if God had spoken to us. The answer was always "no". One evening we went with them to a meeting to hear a visiting overseas speaker by the name of Art Katz, whose tapes Tony had heard and admired. He was a very good preacher, but no word from God came out of the message. A friend of Tony's offered us a job working in a Salvation Army work program for delinquent teenagers. As the week wore on without development Tony picked up on it and asked me if I did not think this offer might be from the Lord. "What is it you want to do" he asked? "I don't know," I replied.

I knew I wanted to serve the Lord, more than anything. I wanted to uncover and follow His plan for my life. But what that was I could not say. Even after more than a year of looking to the Lord for direction I really just did not know. I had looked and considered all the normal avenues of Christian service: being a minister, a missionary, youth work. Not one of them really appealed to me. I felt like a kid leaving school without any idea what to do. More than anything I wanted to serve God, but I couldn't put in words how I wanted to do that. I had the call of God but nowhere to go. I needed to hear from God. Somehow the Holy Spirit needed to bear witness to my spirit.

Later in the week we traveled with Tony to another town, Whangarei, as he wanted to hear Art Katz, whom we had heard earlier in the week in Auckland. An odd thing happened after the service as we were waiting to exit at the door. A lady from the fellowship greeted us and invited us back to her house for lunch. It turned out Art was staying at her house as her guest. She told us later, "I never invite people back for lunch when I have a speaker staying. I don't know quite why I invited you." This was interesting. Maybe God was orchestrating something here. I began to get expectant. It was the first exciting development in a pretty uneventful week. Though we spent a pleasant afternoon in the company of our host and the speaker, still there was no word of direction from God.

What is IT Lord? If you want me to serve *you* I need to hear from you. I was becoming tired of the whole thing. It was getting toward the end of the week, and I wasn't going to give it any longer. I needed to get out and get a job and get on with life; not an exciting prospect but reality. The week had gone by with no word from the Lord, only the Salvation Army job offer. Tony again encouraged us to consider if this might not have been God's direction. To be honest I never for a moment took the offer seriously and never gave it a moment of thought. Because the Lord had not shown anything else, Tony thought we were dismissing it without considering it properly.

"It is ministry, isn't it? And you want to serve God, right?"
"Well yes, but..." I replied.

"It is serving the needy you know, and that is what we are called to do, isn't it?"

"Well yes, but I don't..." I replied again.

"And it is training and you said you wanted an opportunity to be prepared. Who knows what other doors might open up to you with some training and experience behind you!" He concluded by pointing out if I couldn't say what I did want, how could I be sure it was not from God. There was a cold logic to his wisdom that was unanswerable, but left my heart unmoved. Surely if leading a work team of delinquent kids in trouble with the law was my vocation and this were what God wanted me to do, wouldn't I feel a witness in my spirit? Wouldn't it be desirable, something I wanted to do and found challenging? Maybe not. Maybe ministry isn't supposed to be fulfilling. Maybe it is like the army: do this, do that and who cares whether you have an affinity for potatoes, just peel them! Maybe I was not hearing God because I was so fixated with the notion that I should "feel" something.

How do you hear God? When I committed my life to Christ I decided if I was asked to help out in the church or I saw a need I would respond and trust it was God's will. It is a good way to begin in the faith. Every new Christian should make themselves available and useful around the church. Sooner or later, though, you discover not all invitations are of God and if you tried to meet every need there would be no time for family, and so you have to use discernment and turn down some opportunities. Ministry is more than just making yourself useful. You should enjoy ministry. If we are to be effective in ministry it must hold some attraction more than simply filling a need. People who are fulfilled in their lives are those who are doing what God created them to do. I see my cousin, a mechanic by trade, who still loves to tinker with cars even when he is home. I see my son's history teacher whose hobby is studying the Civil War. I see pilots who take their annual holiday to coincide with an airplane show. Their work is their passion. They are drawn to their work because it satisfies some inner sense of identity.

This is true not only in the secular world but the sacred as well. I read about a pastor back in the Depression who saved every penny he could to buy a concordance. I see missionaries on furlough who can't wait to get back to the poverty and privations of a third world country. Some people say they put out a fleece when seeking God's will. One minister I heard once said he told the Lord if he won a religious essay contest he would take it as a sign and become a minister. I often wonder what he would have done if he had lost. Would he have chosen another vocation? Did ministry mean that little to him? I have never trusted in fleeces for guidance. God no doubt has a care and concern for delinquent kids. I could serve His purposes by taking a job working with these kids, but could I be effective if my heart was not in it?

As the week drew to a close I sensed a shift in Tony's attitude toward us. I think he and Denny had come to the conclusion the job offer was God's providential leading. God had spoken and given the direction I sought, and it just remained for me to see it that way. I felt the pressure to say that this was God's leading. Everyone would be happy if I just said, "Ok everybody I believe this job offer is from God and the answer to my search for His leading in my life." Our car of faith had run off the road and now if we just took this job offer and called it an answer to prayer we could get this faith car moving again.

I didn't! Stubbornly I held out. I wanted to hear from God myself, and if I didn't I wasn't going to say I had. My strong feelings were influenced by an experience I had with a person who was part of a small Christian fellowship. Sheryl came to me one day and said she was thinking of selling her home and putting all the money into the fellowship. Her intent was to buy a small trailer for a home and live on the property with others in the fellowship and be part of a community. She felt God wanted her to identify with this church on a much deeper level of commitment. I counseled her that she should not do this unless she were absolutely sure it was God who required it of her. Well, she went ahead, and in the freshness and euphoria of that commitment testified to many people how she had given everything to God and had nothing left she could call her own. Sometime later things went sour, the group broke up and Sheryl wanted all her money back. Her lawyer claimed the community had taken her money by false pretences because they had failed to deliver on a dream. Sheryl would not be the only Christian who has followed a course of action claiming God had spoken to them and then turned around when things have not worked out and blamed someone in the church for leading them astray with faulty counsel. This episode does demonstrate, however, that hearing God is a subjective matter entirely up to the individual concerned. When people say "God spoke to me" or "God led me" or "God showed me," they are usually using the term very loosely. It may not be more than a vague feeling or impression, perhaps some verse of scripture imprinted on their mind. God's leading may not be any more than a set of fortuitous circumstances. Subjective it may be, but that does not mean we can never be sure whether or not God has spoken. As I sought God for direction this episode came to mind and I determined that I was not going to say "God told me" unless I was sure God told me. I believed very strongly then, as I do today, that we use the term far too loosely and in so doing we are guilty of taking the Lord's name in vain. You cannot have it both ways; once you say "God told me," you had better not turn around later if things do not work out and look for someone to blame.

On the last day of the week we had committed to hear from God we went in to pray with Tony and Denny for the last time. Tony asked, "Have you heard from God." When I said "No", he told us to go back out to our trailer and pray about the job offer. No discussion this time, no more counsel. Just get out there and pray. He might as well have said, "Don't waste our time any more with this." We had clearly exhausted his patience. As we walked out the back door of the house toward our trailer, I was troubled and vexed. "Why are others so sure about what God is saying to me and I'm not! How come everyone else knows what God is saying to me except me? Why can't God tell me?" I went on in agitation, "I am not going to say this job offer is from God when I know nothing of the kind." Just as we got to the door of the trailer I stopped and said to Jan, "It's time to end this and move on. I can take this offer and work with the kids. We need work. But it is just a job, nothing more. I am not going to say this is God's call on my life just for the sake of bringing closure to this." I went on without thinking, "If I really said what I wanted to do, it would be to work along side someone in ministry like Art Katz and learn from him. Now that would be fun." I do not know where the words came from. They surprised me even as I uttered them. I had not given thought to the idea before that moment. Jan immediately became animated. "Ben Israel" she said! And then repeated, "Ben Israel, I have had Ben Israel on my mind for a few days now." Ben Israel was the name of Art Katz' ministry in Northern Minnesota. Until that week we had never heard the name. No sooner did Jan finish than I blurted out, " God is sending us to Ben Israel. It is for a time of learning and preparation."

There it was. In a moment, God's will which had been concealed was made known and clear to the point of being specific. Go to America! When Mary the mother of Jesus received the announcement from the angel that she was to have a son who would bear the sins of Israel, she hastened to visit her pregnant cousin Elizabeth. Her greeting caused the unborn child in Elizabeth's womb to leap for joy. That child, of course, was John the Baptist, destined by God to go before Jesus to prepare His coming by calling upon Israel to turn from their sins. This unborn child recognized at the sound of Mary's voice that the hope of Israel for which he (John) had a role and purpose had drawn near, and rejoiced. In this wonderfully representative illustration we see how the Spirit of God bears witness to the heart of the faithful. *"For to us God revealed them through the Spirit; for the Spirit searches all things, even the depths of God" (1 Corinthians 2:10).*

The question is often asked, "How do you know when God has spoken to you?" My answer is, "when the baby leaps in the womb." The unformed babe gestating in our spirit - God's call on our life, until that moment a vague and ineffable yet powerful and undeniable urge - spontaneously leapt for joy. We knew. Without a doubt Jan and I knew. This was IT, and it far exceeded anything we could have imagined. This was what we wanted and did not have the knowledge of until a moment before when the Holy Spirit revealed it. The words tumbled out of our mouths under the unction of the Holy Spirit. I would barely finish speaking and Jan carried on from where I left off. No sooner did she cease speaking than I concluded what the Spirit of God was revealing to our spirit. God had spoken! We stood transfixed on the path outside our trailer.

We didn't say another word, we didn't discuss it, we didn't need to, we knew. Less than two minutes after leaving Tony and Denny we were back in the house telling them we had heard from God. They listened dumbfounded, unable to reconcile the transformation of our ignorance of a few moments before into radiant confidence.

Once we heard God's direction the next step was to tell Art, who by now was in another town some 300 miles away, as the principle speaker at an Easter convention. He was surprised to see us and agreed to give us some time when he heard our reason for being there. Following the morning meeting he visited with us at the motel where we were staying. After hearing us relate how God had shown we were to go to Ben Israel for a time of learning and preparation, he quietly told us it was not possible. He told us he got requests from people all around the world on his ministry travels who believed God was leading them to come to his ministry. "What makes you think you are any different?" he asked. He concluded by telling us Ben Israel was a Christian community, not a school. They had no facilities for teaching, nor was there any place for students to stay.

Jan and I had not anticipated a negative response. We assumed since God had shown us we were to go to this ministry then God would have done the same with Art, who headed up the ministry, or at least prepared the way so he would be receptive to the idea. We were caught off guard, but as we made our way to the evening meeting that night we both agreed we had heard from God and should carry on. It would be a long time before we got to Ben Israel, more than two years later, and there would be many turns in the road, many twists before it came about. Had we not heard God for ourselves I doubt we would have lasted.

You have to hear God for yourself. Unfortunately some

Christians have never sought God for themselves. They run to the pastor for advice when the best advice he could give them is to go away and get a word from the Lord for themselves. Nobody can say what God is speaking to you, except you. You can not turn this responsibility over to someone else. It is not possible to have overcoming faith if you are only acting on the advice of others. For in speaking, God not only directs us but more importantly His speaking births within in us the desire to do His bidding. His will becomes our hope. From the moment God spoke telling us to go to Ben Israel Ministries, getting to America became the focus of our life.

Taking Ourselves Seriously

chapter three

Standing alongside the minister in front of the church during a Sunday service were some members of the congregation. On the spur of the moment he asked them to give a short impromptu testimony. When it came to the turn of one man he begged off saying, "I don't know why I am up here. I am no one special. I am just a very ordinary man." I heard something in my spirit that said this was not right. I sensed this was a man who had never taken himself seriously as a Christian. Since at any given moment the opportunity to bear witness to Christ our Lord and Savior may present itself, we should be ready at all times to do so. This man shirked his obligation and responsibility before God with the excuse he was unworthy. That may seem like humility, when in fact he was denying the efficacy of Christ's sacrifice.

In the act of calling us to be a witness God also qualified us - *"But you are a chosen race, a royal priesthood, a holy nation, a people for God's own possession, that you may proclaim the excellencies of Him who has called you out of darkness into His marvelous light" (1 Peter 2:9).*

We are chosen! I wonder how many regular churchgoers consider themselves chosen. The more common practice is to describe ourselves by our church affiliation and refer to ourselves as a member of such and such a church. Nothing too much is expected from members other than to show up regularly for meetings, and unfortunately for some Believers that is about as far as it goes in meeting their obligation before God. We are never going to be an effective witness for Christ until we change the way we see ourselves to conform with the terms Peter uses to describe how God sees us. With that thought in mind let us look more closely at what it means to be a Christian.

"I come in the name of the Lord."

Most Christians are ordinary men and women holding down jobs and raising families. I head for work in my car, fighting the traffic like everyone else. Arriving at work I am just another face in the crowd. Nothing sets me apart from those around me: I am dressed much the same as everyone else, I do the same work as my coworkers, taking my instructions from the same boss. God's word says I am special, but the world says I am Joe Average. So far as being set apart for God's own possession is concerned, everything about my life tends to emphasize my solidarity with mankind. I face the same issues as anyone else at my stage in life: buying a house, balancing my check book, trying to be a good parent and raise good kids. If I were older the issues would probably be health care and the price of prescription drugs. Like most of my contemporaries at work I'm looking forward to the weekend and planning my summer vacation. We Christians are ordinary men and women caught up in the same pursuits as our unbelieving

Taking Ourselves Seriously

neighbors. Those things that make for joy and sorrow in their lives touch our lives too. We're like everyone else and at the same time we are not like everyone else. We are set apart for God's use. We are in the crowd yet apart from the crowd. We are special, not because of who we are, but because of whom we represent - Christ.

In the midst of the mundane everyday stuff of life are opportunities to do the works of God by those who see themselves as representatives of God. David was on an errand to take food to his brothers who were soldiers in Sauls' army fighting the Philistines when he heard Goliath's taunts against Israel's army. We are all familiar with the story of how this young shepherd boy, untrained as a soldier, went up against his formidable battle-hardened foe armed with no more than a slingshot. What gave him the courage? Listen to what he said as he approached his foe:

"You come to me with a sword, a spear, and a javelin, but I come to you in the name of the LORD of hosts, the God of the armies of Israel, whom you have taunted. This day the LORD will deliver you up into my hands, and I will strike you down and remove your head from you. And I will give the dead bodies of the army of the Philistines this day to the birds of the sky and the wild beasts of the earth, that all the earth may know that there is a God in Israel" (1 Sam 17:45,46).

David saw himself as a part of the people of God. He so identified with God that he took Goliath's taunts of Israel as an affront against God. In going up against Goliath David represented God and as God's emissary confidently expected God to deliver Goliath into his hand. In your daily comings and goings do you see yourself coming in the name of the Lord? Do you see yourself as His emissary prepared and ready to represent Him if the occasion should arise? There are opportunities to witness for Christ every day. To take advantage of them we must, like David, come to the place where we see ourselves as a people for God's own possession.

A holy nation. A royal priesthood.

So far as being holy is concerned the word is likely to make many of us run our finger uncomfortably around our collar. I watched a television documentary about some Russian orphans who had been adopted by American families. Some of these kids proved too difficult for their adopted families to handle and they returned them to the placement agency. The agency in turn placed a lot of these unmanageable children with a Christian couple who were willing to take them in and foster them. The kids responded to the loving patience of this family and turned out to be happy, well adjusted children. By contrasting their present home life with footage shot earlier in their lives you could see the remarkable transformation in these kids. The interviewer said to the husband at the end, "You are a saint!" To which the man replied "No I am not, far from it." But he is! That is exactly what he is - a saint.

Many of the new testament letters you read are addressed 'to the saints,' - Romans, Corinthians, Ephesians, Philippians, to name a few. So far as the apostle Paul is concerned every person who calls Jesus Christ their Lord and Savior is a saint. Unfortunately in modern day usage we have come to understand a "saint" as an especially devout person who has led an exceptional life of such singular devotion and self sacrifice that even the closest scrutiny can not turn up any fault or flaw to mar their image of purity. Most people's idea of a saint is someone like Mother Theresa. In order to qualify as this kind of

Taking Ourselves Seriously 43

saint, you need to remain celibate, join a religious order, renounce all worldly possessions, then go and live in India and work with the untouchables in the slums. Saints are so rare hardly any are left alive, they're all dead!

This conventional understanding of sainthood is a merit-based concept, the very antithesis of the biblical teaching of an imputed righteousness by faith. It undermines the effective witness of the majority of Christians. Ordinary men and women who hold down a job or are busy at home raising a family lack spiritual self esteem. One woman confided, "I struggle with this feeling of being unworthy. I am busy doing housework and looking after children and get the thought I should pray for someone, and I think "Oh no, I haven't read the bible yet today." We need to contend for the original biblical definition of a saint as anyone who confesses Jesus as Lord.

It was this idealized notion of sainthood that lay behind the remark a brother in the Lord made when he told me, "You couldn't have TV and be a minister." When I asked "Why not?" he replied, "What if someone knocked on your door Monday night and needed ministry?" His reasoning, it seems, was that the activity of watching football was not conducive to maintaining a proper spiritual state of mind. He might as well have said you cannot be a minister and do your taxes, or plan a romantic evening with your wife. Either of those activities would necessitate a radical change in our mind set if interrupted by a knock on our door by someone who wanted counseling!

Those who view a saint as some exceptional Christian persist in this romantic view that saints do not deal with the issues of life as ordinary men and women, but in their devotion to God have managed to detach themselves from the mundane things of life. The myth persists of a holy man who lives on the top of a hill far removed from all human contact. Periodically he comes down from his lofty place led by his disciples. He has a towel carefully wrapped around his eyes so he will not see anything profane along the way that might affect his mystical union with God and compromise his mission to deliver God's word to the masses. The greater the degree of separation and detachment from the world the more effective is the 'priest'. It is true the word 'holiness' carries the idea of separation, but that did not mean putting distance between yourself and your fellow men and all human activity. It meant distinguishing the sacred from the profane and not mixing the two. In the old testament only the High Priest could enter the holy of holies in the temple where the presence of the Lord was, and then only once a year. But the high priest was chosen from among men. He approached God from the midst of men, not on some holy hill. The reason a priest ministers effectively on behalf of men is that he knows their weaknesses. He is like men, he is a man, and comes from the midst of men. He is engaged in the same pursuits as other men. Their struggle is his struggle, their temptations are his temptations. Their hopes and aspirations are his. He loves, he dreams, he cries. It is because he knows the struggle men are engaged in that he can sacrifice on their behalf. He can make intercession effectively because he is familiar with the frailties of men.

By His grace under the new Covenant God calls you and me as priests and has given us access to His throne of grace to petition Him on behalf of needy men and women any time night or day. We may not wear the garb of a clergyman by which priests are usually recognized. But we are probably the only priests the majority of the unbelieving people we work with will ever have contact with. If we do not take the initiative in regard to our calling as priest's seriously we will miss the opportunities that occur to mediate between mankind and God.

In the world where people are hurting, we have the word of God, a real comfort. When people have lost hope, we know of an anchor in a stormy sea. When people are in darkness and do not know which way to turn, we are light bearers. When the world needs answers, we know the One who is called Counselor. When the down-trodden and oppressed have nowhere to turn, we can lead them to God.

Maybe the biggest psychological hurdle we face in taking ourselves seriously as Christians' is that so often we do not feel holy. The problem is living like a son of God when you feel like a son of man. The bleary-eyed vacant face staring back at me from the mirror as I shave in the morning is a far cry from the beatific expression one associates with holiness. It would be a supreme act of will to even summon up a spiritual thought as I run the razor over my day old stubble. The only thing on my mind right now is the harsh words I spoke in anger last night to my son which I am regretting right now. "Who are you kidding? You think you are God's man. Ha, what a joke!" the image in the mirror sneers. He knows me, this man in the mirror in the mornings. I can't refute him. I agree. Not me. I cannot be spoken of in the same breath as real men of God. I have let God down, again! It is not the first time I have lost my temper with my son. I just can't seem to get the victory and be the father I want to be. Who am I to tell other people about righteousness?

But read the stories as recorded in the Bible of the men and women of faith and you soon see they had personal failings. Their character was sometimes marked by serious defects and flaws as in the case of David, whose treatment of Uriah was one of the most selfish and sinful acts recorded in the Bible. Yet he is described in the Bible as a man after God's heart. He had family problems, did David: he was a dysfunctional father whose own child rose against him;

another son murdered his brother. In the midst of this he could compose some of the most beautiful psalms to encourage those afflicted and weighed down with sin and guilt, because he spoke out of his own experience.

Look at Sarah, who laughed in unbelief when told she would have a son. Yet Sarah is listed among the great faith hero's in the book of Hebrews. The faith heroes in the Bible were not suited to their role because of their extraordinary moral character. They were just very ordinary men and women with character flaws doing extraordinary things for God because they were over comers. When I hear a Christian with the opportunity to proclaim the excellencies of God saying, "I don't know what I am doing up here," I know they are looking in the mirror and not the word of God. The opportunity to serve God may come fresh on the heels of our own personal failure and from a profound sense of unworthiness. To be able to say, "I come in the name of the Lord," under those circumstances requires real faith.

Are you beginning to see yourself as chosen by God, a royal priesthood set apart to minister to men and women? A holy person who can call yourself a saint? A person for God's own possession? Are you beginning to grasp how great is our calling and what degree of responsibility God has entrusted toward us? Can you picture yourself alongside the great faith heroes of the Bible without wincing in embarrassment? You may think I am overstating the case. Then listen to this - *"because God had provided something better for us, so that apart from us they should not be made perfect" (Hebrews 11:40).* The writer just listed all the faith heroes of the Bible; Abraham, Noah, Isaac, and then linked these great men and women with the faithful who were the recipients of the letter to the Hebrews. It is a staggering thought to contemplate, yet it holds true:

the works of faith these great men and women identified in Hebrews chapter eleven did, greatly advanced God's kingdom purposes, yet it is not complete without our contribution. You and I are part of a continuum of saints down the ages that began with Abraham. So far as God is concerned we are right up there with all the faith heroes listed in the Bible.

'I am the man.'

Going into the 1993 world series Philadelphia's form player was Lenny Dykstra. His prowess with the bat in clutch situations was a major reason Philadelphia had done so well. Hunched aggressively over the plate he took the pitchers deep into the count, made them throw him a strike and then swung on it for a home run. A reporter interviewing Lenny commented on his form and suggested that without his presence in the lineup his team's chances of winning were significantly less. His reply was classic - "What can I say? I am the man." Now there's self confidence for you. Not the false modesty we might have expected; "Aw shucks, I'm just lucky I guess." Lenny acknowledged the remark as a simple statement of truth.

It is good to be chosen. To be the player everyone wants on their team. Lenny knew his worth to the team. What's more he was comfortable with the expectations his teammates and fans placed on him. That God has chosen us is the thing to keep in mind. I am not in the church because one day I became a member. I am in the church because God chose me. The idea that God has chosen us is expressed time and again throughout the Bible. When reference is made in the Old Testament regarding Israel's unique place among the nations, it is in terms of their being chosen. In the New Testament the disciples who follow Christ are chosen. Those who come to believe in Him after His death do so because they are drawn by the Holy Spirit. We did not choose God, He chose us. We commonly use terms such as a person 'accepts Christ' as if it were up to us whether or not we become a Christian; or, we might say a person makes 'a decision for Christ', suggesting we took the first step toward religion. It is not so. The initiative for our salvation lay with God. He chose us.

What can I say then except to admit like Lenny, "I am the man." I am God's man. Yes I am. When the situation arises and God's interests are involved, I hope I will not hesitate, because God has placed me there for this very occasion. I am God's man for the hour, and I had better know it. When the man says, "I do not know why I am up here, I am just an ordinary man," he establishes a connection with ninety per cent of the audience; but not with God. We might impress others with our false modesty, but God is offended by it. When Jeremiah was called by God to be a prophet to the nations he protested that he was too young to speak and didn't know how. His low self esteem earned the prophet a serious rebuke.

Most of us are not important in the world. Israel was chosen as God's people precisely because they were a small insignificant nation. Remember, the greatest king in Israel, David, was chosen last of his brothers. He was overlooked altogether by his father when he paraded his sons before Samuel, the prophet who had come to anoint a son of Jesse as king. But David was God's choice. God deliberately chose us, and for the same reason. We are not important in the eyes of the world: *"For consider your calling, brethren, that there were not many wise according to the flesh, not many mighty, not many noble; but God has chosen the foolish things of the world to shame the wise, and God has chosen the weak things of the world to shame the things which are strong"* (1 Corinthians 1:26,27).

Every day we go about our daily affairs our ordinariness is in our face. There is a choice before us - either we live up to our high calling, or down to the esteem we are held in by the world.

Men of Faith Don't Whine!

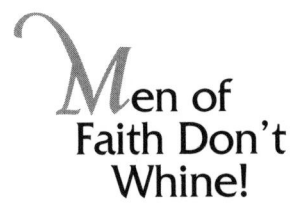

chapter four

Blessed is the man who trusts in the Lord And whose trust is the Lord.

For he will be like a tree planted by the water, That extends its roots by a stream And will not fear when the heat comes; But its leaves will be green, And it will not be anxious in a year of drought Nor cease to yield fruit.

The heart is more deceitful than all else And is desperately sick; Who can understand it?

I, the LORD, search the heart, I test the mind, Even to give to each man according to his ways, According to the results of his deeds.

(Jeremiah 17:7-10)

The prophet Jeremiah gives a wonderful description of a man who trusts God. He will be like a tree planted by the water whose roots go down to the stream. When the heat comes and there's a drought, that tree's leaf will still be green and it will not cease to yield fruit. The distinctive mark of personal faith is a moral character that bears up under adversity. Long-suffering, love, joy, self-control, patience, peace, kindness, goodness are some of the moral qualities listed in the Bible as the fruit of the Spirit. The list is by no means exclusive. We could add honesty, loyalty, courage. These admirable qualities constitute godly character and should be readily apparent in men and women of faith at all times and under all circumstances, in good times as well as bad.

We can all show love when we are in harmony with others. It is easy to be peaceful when you are not married and have no kids. Patience isn't a virtue when you are on course and moving ahead toward the goals in your life. There is nothing remarkable about extending kindness toward people we care about, or being joyful when we get a promotion at work or pass an exam at school. A generosity of spirit and good temper are not hard to come by when we are winning at life. Sometimes, though, the circumstances of life are not to our liking and unless our moral behavior is grounded in something deeper than good fortune it tends to break down. Although Art Katz had discouraged us in our attempt to travel to the USA and spend time with his ministry he did not shut the door entirely. At his suggestion we wrote to Ben Israel ministries telling them about ourselves and why we felt called of the Lord to go there. Subsequently in their next newsletter sent to Tony and Denny was the following announcement:

"Since my return home the Lord seems to be impressing us to establish a training school for end-time ministries of a prophetic kind. We hope to be working on the physical aspect of that this summer in that the Lord has provided an inexpensive building to be relocated on our property this summer."

At the bottom of the page was a handwritten note:

"Perhaps this is the answer for Ken and Jan to be among the first class - January 1983. Though we are contemplating a four month curriculum, the prospect of their remaining on with us after that would be very good."

We were overjoyed! God had confirmed His word to us. We had the go-ahead to proceed. We even had a date, January 1983. As Jan and I waited to fulfill God's call on our life to go to America, we set out to save enough for our air fares and support ourselves overseas for about a year. We took whatever work we could find, usually low paid temporary work and, in the depressed economy of the time, very irregular. We rented a mobile home in a trailer park which we had to vacate every holiday season when the landlord could command a higher price. Ours was a very transient lifestyle, without a permanent address or regular job. I counted thirteen changes of address in one year during this period, and more dead end jobs than I care to remember.

I was becoming discouraged. The time for the school to start had come and gone and we hadn't heard from the ministry in America since their initial communication. Beyond a brief statement in one of their rare newsletters that the planned school for overseas students, to which we were invited, was delayed, we had heard nothing further. It was taking longer than I expected. Each temporary job I took I told myself, "Before I finish working here some development will have taken place. Surely we will hear from them with some firm dates for starting the school." But we never did, not even so much as a letter to update us on the progress they were making.

Each day the first thing I did on arrival home from work was to look and see if a letter had arrived. The exciting thought that we were going to America for 'a time of learning and preparation' brightened each day in the rather monotonous temporary jobs I had. Each evening's ritual mail box scenario brought a temporary disappointment. The letter that never came became the focal point of my life.

One job I had in particular stands out during that time, that of working for a large nursery. The boss' son, curious to know more about my desire to go to America, began questioning me. "Why are you going? When are you going?" I took the opportunity to share a little about how God had led us. It didn't make a lot of sense to him. I could tell he had no real concept of a God who directs people's lives. As his questioning progressed and elicited from me the fact that the school I wanted to go to didn't exist yet and very little of my trip was cut and dried, his skepticism became more and more apparent. I spoke honestly and openly from my heart, only to see my efforts to communicate received with a blank look that gave way to open contempt.

It is miserable working in jobs that mean nothing to you when you would far rather be doing something else. But you can bear it if it accomplishes a goal. You tell yourself, "Just a little longer and I will be out of here." If you aren't making progress toward the goal and others undermine your resolve by questioning your judgement, then it becomes intolerable.

The work in the nursery was mostly in glasshouses and it was hot and hard. As a temporary employee not expected to remain, I got all the undesirable jobs. If it involved digging in hot glasshouses, or shifting piles of potting mix, I did it. I was the low person on the totem pole. I was nothing, a nobody, expendable, simply someone to be taken advantage of and used as long as I was around. And if I didn't like it there were plenty of others in the depressed economy available to take my place. I hated the boss. A miserable, humorless person who barely noticed me, always directing my tasks for the day by having another employee instruct me. Previously I had had my own business growing tomatoes and cucumbers in glasshouses...from glasshouse proprietor to glasshouse laborer. The irony of this was not lost on me and Satan used it to mock my aspirations. I was the prodigal son who had it good and squandered his inheritance. "You're kidding yourself that you're going to America. You aren't going anywhere. This is where your hope has brought you and this is where it all ends up," he whispered as I bent double in ninety degree heat shoveling dirt.

One intolerably hot day in the middle of digging trenches in a glasshouse, it all caught up with me, my unfair treatment in getting all the worst jobs, the fact that I was not saving any money from my meager wage, nor seeing any developments in my quest to go to America. I was strongly tempted to throw the shovel I held right through the glasshouse and just quit. Oh boy, was I tempted! That moment is still with me after all these years. Maybe the boss' son had it right, I was a fool. Maybe it was time to find a regular job and close the door on America and get on with life. It is vexing to have a hope and feel you are not moving toward it. All the energy you muster to move ahead has no effect whatsoever; and the single-mindedness of purpose you bring to bear avails nothing. It is not simply a problem that can be solved by a quick fix, but a state of affairs you have no control over. This is definitely not living the dream. It is not how we imagined it would be when we set out on the journey.

There is a reason why glasshouse stuff happens. The Bible passage we are looking at tells us what that purpose is: *"The heart is more deceitful than all else And is desperately sick; Who can understand it? I, the LORD, search the heart" (Jeremiah 17:9,10).* The heart! The unseen influence of our life - the source and fount of who and what a man really is - the heart. And it is deceitful, desperately sick, unreliable. Only in adversity does the personality of the heart reveal it's true colors.

There is a name for glasshouse stuff. The bible calls it trials, and scripture leaves us in no doubt whatsoever that our faith will be tested in this way. It is by way of trials that our heavenly Father molds our character. Character is not something we are born with. Nor is it acquired at conversion when we are born again from above. Character cannot be acquired during one hour of church on Sunday, or accumulated hours of Bible study. You won't find character listed as one of the gifts of the Spirit. Godly character does not come to us directly from God, but indirectly - a fruit of the Spirit to be worked out in us as a response to the vicissitudes of life.

"For they disciplined us for a short time as seemed best to them, but He disciplines us for our good, that we may share His holiness. All discipline for the moment seems not to be joyful, but sorrowful; yet to those who have been trained by it, afterwards it yields the peaceful fruit of righteousness" (Hebrews 12:10,11).

Those provocation's in our life we find unbearable and vexing are God's way of training us in righteousness. Though unpleasant and disagreeable, they are in God's view a necessary discipline designed to conform us to His own character. If there is fundamental integrity and strong moral character the challenges of life will ultimately bring out the best in us. If not, the trial will expose the true motives of our heart. 'The tree's leaf will still be green and it will not cease to yield fruit, even in a drought.' God says, "I'm going to put Ken here to work in this nursery. It's not at all what he expects and it is going to confound him. Even humiliate him. But I want to see fruit from his life at this time. I want to see him walk with joy and peace in his heart and continued faith in me. I want to see patience and long-suffering as proof his faith is alive and well." The man who trusts in the Lord will not wilt or wither in a time of adversity but continue to bear fruit.

That hot day in the glasshouse leaning on my shovel I did some hard thinking. I had let myself become a victim of my circumstances. I had allowed the unfavorable conditions to turn me bitter. My normal joy and good humor had been replaced by negativity and self-pity. I was feeling sorry for myself. "No one is keeping you here, Ken" I told myself. "You can leave any time you want, or you can choose to stay. But whether you stay or leave you need to change your attitude." The revelation that came to me as I thought about my unhappy state of affairs was this: my complaining spirit was a sign I was not yielded to God. Men of faith don't whine!

I asked myself if I still believed in my heart that God had called me to America and if I was still committed to this course. The answer on both counts was 'yes.' I knew if I was ever going to get to America then I had to change my attitude to reflect faith. I chose to carry on with America as my goal. I rededicated my life to God, placed my hopes in His hands and determined simply to trust Him. Whatever happened, I determined to change my attitude. Though conditions at work did not change, I did.

Sometime later I came into the lunch room and the two girls were there having lunch. "What have you been doing this morning, Ken?" they asked. "Swimming in the boss' pool," I replied straight-faced. The boss, my nemesis, had his house at the back of the property with a swimming pool in the yard. Looking at my hot grimy face they burst out laughing. After that it became a standing joke, one which I embellished. I had the boss serving me drinks as I lay in his hammock beside the pool. "Ken, can I get you anything else?" I mimicked the boss. The girls would howl with laughter at the image it evoked. Throughout that summer the question, "Ken what have you been doing?" was a signal for me to wax lyrical. In the end the boss was my servant, at my every beck and call, fetching me towels after a swim, while I relaxed beside the pool, moving my chair for me to a shadier spot. I would rebuke him if he was too slow and he would apologize. It made for some light entertainment. I got on well there after that. I was relaxed, I was my old self again, and conditions even got better. It seemed to me I was doing more variety in the work, not so much of the heavy grunt stuff.

The previously distant autocratic boss even seemed a bit more human, not so aloof. One day he came up to me and said another young man who had just completed a horticulture course at university had approached him for an apprenticeship. He told me there was enough work to justify making my temporary job permanent, but only enough work for one person. If I wanted the job he would turn the other person down and make me a full time employee. There was only one stipulation; he knew all about my desire to go overseas, so if I wanted the job I would have to commit to a year, since the student was willing to sign on and do an apprenticeship. Not knowing when the school in America might start I couldn't give him a year's commitment, so I left.

They threw a surprise party for me on my last day. Unknown to me the girls had told everyone else *as well as the boss* about our little joke. To my chagrin and everyone else's delight he came into the lunch room carrying a big cake and drinks and proceeded to make a big fuss of serving me, acting out in good humor the servant I had made him out to be. I had gotten the victory over my attitude by the time I left. It was not a stoical grit your teeth and smile but a real inner transformation. I was genuinely sorry to leave. When things don't go right we wonder if God is angry with us. Maybe He is punishing us. Or perhaps we don't measure up and are being rejected. But the trial is not punishment, it is training. It is because we are sons and daughters of the Living God that we go through trials - not because we have gotten outside his love and care. Trials are inevitable to anyone who calls themselves a Believer; *"for those whom the Lord loves he disciplines, and he scourges every son whom He receives" (Hebrews 12:6).*

We need a fresh revelation that God has placed us where we are and that we are to bear fruit there. Instead of focusing on trying to escape our circumstances, we need to concentrate on trying to handle them. It is not to say we shouldn't look to change our circumstances. We can pray and ask God for things we see as fundamental to our happiness. But prospering ought not to be the prerequisite for our fruitfulness.

A trial is going to make us a better person or a worse person: *"Consider it all joy, my brethren, when you encounter various trials"* the Bible says. To an unbeliever this does not make any sense. Trials are what cause them aggravation and frustration, typically bringing forth the deeds of the flesh - anger, jealousy, bitterness, envy, and resentment. However, the rest of the verse goes on to explain why Christians should consider unpleasant circumstances a cause for rejoicing - *"knowing that the testing of your faith produces endurance. And let endurance have its perfect result, that you may be perfect and complete, lacking in nothing." (James 1:2-4).* What is trouble for the unbeliever is training in righteousness for the Believer. If you value godly character then you can thank God for trials. Those whose trust is in the Lord are enabled to withstand hardship knowing the end result is worthwhile, no less than conformity to God's own character. Holiness!

"The steps of a good man are established by the LORD; And He delights in his way "(Psalm 37:23).

There is an old adage that says character is destiny. Whether our plans and aspirations for the future are established by God depends upon whether our moral behavior can stand up to adversity in the present. God detests whiners. Such people have no reason to expect from God what they are looking for.

In the scriptures we have been looking at God states this emphatically: *"I, the LORD, search the heart...to give to each man according to his ways"...(Jeremiah 17:10).* A whole generation of Israel perished in the wilderness because every time they found themselves in trouble they complained. God equated their grumbling with unbelief. He continually tested them but their faint hearts led them astray. He would not allow them to enter the promised land. Israel did not see in the hidden test of their circumstances an opportunity to glorify God.

We cannot control what happens to us, but we can do something about our response. I see those in the church who are always dispirited. Trials have not worked character in them. Instead adversity has exposed their lack of faith. It is not the fruit of the Spirit that is being manifest in the crucible of affliction but rather the deeds of the flesh: resentment, anger, indifference, jealousy. Life is unreasonably hard for them, they are not seeing the results they would like from life that make for happiness and fervently wish their misfortune would turn. That state of affairs is unlikely as long as God equates character with faith. They fail to appreciate that the troublesome things are happening to them so God can be exalted. Their failure to respond positively to God's testing precludes the favor of God who gives *"to each man according to his ways, According to the results of his deeds."*

Sometimes the road we are travelling looks nothing like the destination and we question if it's taking us anywhere. We look at our goals and worry about where we will be a year from now. We want to make the leap now and be done.

Men of Faith Don't Whine!

But it is steps that get us to our goal, not leaps, and each step is an act of faith. We tend to categorize glasshouse stuff as an aberration, a fork in the road that took us nowhere. God reassures us from His word that all our steps are under His control and leading us toward His purpose for our life. Eventually I went to America, spending a year at the Bible school. Yes, my plans were established by the Lord. Those of us who have been down the road a little further can reassure those starting out and finding themselves pressed down and hemmed in from all sides that they are on the right road. We can look back at such steps in our own journey and say God got us here, and He got us here in good shape.

We make faith the means to an end, when from God's perspective our faith is an end in itself. There is a line in a chorus we sing that makes this point, "The highway to your city runs through my heart." Reaching our destination is not so much about being in the right place at the right time as it is about being in the right frame of mind. From our point of view it is important to us we reach the destination, while from God's point of view it is important we reach it in the right condition.

Poolside and Rooftop

chapter five

> *Now there is in Jerusalem by the sheep gate a pool, which is called in Hebrew Bethesda, having five porticoes.*
> *And a certain man was there, who had been thirty-eight years in his sickness.*
> *When Jesus saw him lying there, and knew that he had already been a long time {in that condition,} He said to him, "Do you wish to get well?"*
> **(John 5:2,5,6)**

Periodically the waters in this pool would stir. It was generally believed the phenomenon was caused by an angel and whoever was first in when this happened would be healed. Each motion of the waters set up a rush by the assembled people, all of whom suffered from some affliction or ailment, to be first into the water.

Among the many gathered by the pool Jesus singles one man out and approaching him asks, "Do you wish to get well?" It would seem Jesus was asking the obvious. Clearly the man wanted to be healed, as did the blind man next to him and the sick one over there. We might be tempted to pass right over Jesus' remark, assuming it to be no more than a literary device of the author to launch into his story. Yet John, the writer of this gospel would not have included this question for his readers unless it had some significance, for he observes that Jesus knew the man had been a long time in his condition. Evidently Jesus felt the need to question this man's desire to be healed, even though his condition and presence at the pool would seem to suggest his eagerness.

The man's reply is revealing; "Sir I have no man to put me into the pool when the water is stirred up, but while I am coming, another steps down before me." I suspect he is used to telling this tale of woe to every one who inquires about him. You can almost hear the resignation and tinge of self pity in the voice of this man, who, unable of his own accord to get into the pool, is dependent upon others who have never acted quickly enough for his purposes. At different times in years gone by there's been a shout, a commotion of activity; he's felt himself lifted up, jostled with the other pallets down the steps and into the pool only to look over and see someone else made it into the bubbling waters ahead of him. "Maybe next time" he sighs and settles back down on his pallet to await the next stirring of the waters.

On occasion over the years I've heard the echo of that sigh in Christians I've encountered, and watched the bubbling waters subside over their desires. I've heard it in the forlorn voice of women who have felt trapped in an unfulfilled marriage to husbands who don't share their enthusiasm for the church. I've heard the sigh of lonely single people who don't find the fellowship they crave from other Christians. There are many people in the church with a sigh and their own unique tale of woe. I run across frustrated people who want to be used in ministry but have

Poolside and Rooftop

never really found their niche in the church. One couple I knew had long felt a desire to serve on the mission field. A lack of financial support kept them from going and their predicament was made harder to bear as the husband felt trapped in a low income job he hated. "Perhaps God will open the door next year," the wife wistfully remarked to me from their back door one fall evening.

For these people life falls far short of their expectations. The potential for something greater exists but isn't being realized. Life has not worked out for them in such a way as to fulfill their dreams and the weight of that disappointment is reflected in their voice. I've come away disturbed after an encounter with them, not knowing quite what the solution is to their situation, but at the same time sensing they are too passive in the face of their misfortune. I hesitate to add to their misery by suggesting there is more they can do for themselves, yet after leaving them I cannot avoid the impression they will never achieve the breakthrough they hope for so long as they carry on as they are. Their motivation is not all it can be. Something is very wrong when a Christian's life resounds to the echo of a sigh. If faith is the assurance of things hoped for, why the sigh?

Jesus knew why the man lay near the pool all day - the need in this mans life was obvious - but Jesus saw something in this man that made Him question whether the man's actions reflected faith. "Do you wish to get well?" Jesus asked him. The proper response is a resounding affirmation, "Yes! Oh yes, more than anything I want to get well." A desire that has lost it's power to excite is no longer a real desire.

A sigh is an involuntary groan of the heart - a wrenching exclamation wrung from the inner man trying to bear up under the press of stronger forces. I have come to realize from personal experience that whenever there is a sigh in my voice it means my faith and my hope are not synchronized. I might tell myself and others I am trusting in God, but a sigh is the evidence my faith is not a buttress for the hope within my heart. I might tell myself that I just need to be patient and God will in His time and in His way work it all out. But the sigh tells me in my heart of hearts I am not convinced. Don't ever ignore the sigh, for this important reason: it comes straight from the heart. The sigh is undeniable and irrefutable proof that the Holy Spirit is not comforting my spirit. Whatever I may say to the contrary, the truth is that faith is not underpinning my hope.

Let's give this man at the pool a name, 'Poolside.' It's apt since his life is inextricably linked to the activity taking place in the pool. Each stirring of the water arouses a sense of anticipation in Poolside which lasts only so long as the waters are moving. Apart from periodic bursts of excitement occasioned by the stirring waters he lies inert on his pallet. When the waters are not moving, neither is he. From this observation we can make a further deduction concerning Poolside's level of desire: his hope is not energizing him. It takes an external stimulus to rouse him. All is not well with Poolside's desire, as Jesus rightly knew.

If the pool were an analogy for the church it would accurately replicate modern day Poolsides and their frustrated desires. They look to the church to take the lead and usually are unwilling themselves to take any initiative. They are content to simply mark time, holding their breath as each new speaker appears on the church scene, wondering if perhaps this might be the breakthrough they've patiently waited for. They watch each move of God in their midst with anticipation thinking something might develop which will benefit them, and when it doesn't they experience the same cycle of intense activity followed by a prolonged period of inertia that characterized Poolsides' existence. This lack of motivation raises a serious question regarding their desire: what sort of a hope is it that results in lassitude instead of vigor? The answer is very simple: it is not a real hope at all. Hope enthuses, hope gives vitality. Above all, hope empowers. Someone who is content to wait for the water to stir over their sluggish desires doesn't have a great deal of hope.

Therefore we must raise the question as to whether Poolside really has a desire to walk again. I think he may have once, but I suspect he has now come to terms with his infirmity and resigned himself to his condition. I think his desire to be healed is little more than a wish dream, pleasantly contemplative but uninspiring. He fantasizes about one day walking to the top of the Mount of Olives, or going up with all the pilgrims to celebrate the Passover in Jerusalem. These thoughts relieve the monotony of his life, but aren't a motivating force. The trouble is he has been sick too long. Not only have the muscles in his body atrophied for lack of exercise, but his desire has as well. Proverbs 13:12 in a psychological observation says, *"Hope deferred makes the heart sick, But desire fulfilled is a tree of life."* It has taken too long for Poolside to achieve his ambition and the irony is that the non fulfillment of Poolside's hope has reduced his life to little more than an existence. He is little better off than someone who has no hope at all. John Steinbeck's book, Of Mice And Men, tells the story of two itinerant farm laborers who dream of one day owning their own piece of land and 'living off the fat of the land.' It's not going to happen, the reader knows this, and deep down at least one of the characters probably knows it too. Nevertheless, he maintains the illusion for his simple minded partner because the self deception serves to promote the facade that his life has meaning and purpose. You can get used to living this way.

You might think I'm being hard on Poolside; after all, the poor guy is unable to walk. What else can he do but sit around and wait. So what if the years have taken the edge off his desire. Surely his prolonged wait beside the pool demonstrates conclusively he has put all his faith in God? On the surface Poolside's lengthy sojourn in anticipation of a miracle would seem to suggest he has faith in God to meet his need, but let's take a closer look.

One thing to note about Poolside which is revealed in response to Jesus' question is that he holds the view his failure to be healed is due to the absence of anyone willing or able to get him into the pool when the waters are being stirred. Poolside is quite convinced there is nothing he himself can do to help his cause and makes no effort to do so. He has come to depend upon others. Although the stirring of the waters is the consequence of a Divine action, yet in the first instance someone else has to act in order for Poolside to be healed. I've observed in my encounters with those whose lives are a sigh, that though they claim to be looking to God and trusting Him for the breakthrough in their lives, in reality they are looking toward other people in the church to bring about their change of fortune. Often they are critical of people in the church for not being as zealous as they would like, the leadership for not sharing their vision, or the pastor for not being anointed. It is typical of these people to be attracted to personalities in the church who seem to offer them the opportunity for ministry. As one couple move to yet another new church, the wife mentions that the pastor didn't keep his promise to use her husband's spiritual gifts. "But the new pastor has a similar vision to ours and has said he can really use someone like us in the church." After an interval of some years I will meet them again, leaving that church for another

Poolside and Rooftop

and expressing similar optimism for the next church and disillusionment with the one they've just left. Like Poolside they've become dependent upon other people who never act decisively or quickly enough for them.

Something else makes me question the extent to which Poolside is placing his faith in God. Let's go back and become bystanders in this little drama enacted two thousand years ago. Poolside is lying upon his pallet when Jesus approaches and asks if he wants to get well. Listen carefully to his reply to Jesus: "Sir, I have no man to put me into the pool when the water is stirred up, but while I am coming another steps down before me." Imagine the scene if you can, look at it in your mind and ask the question: "What is wrong with this picture?" The moment Poolside has waited thirty eight years for has arrived; at Jesus simple command, "Arise, take up your pallet and walk," he will do so. Jesus the healer is standing beside him. Yet he is still looking in the direction of the pool. The pool won't play any part whatsoever in this man's healing and yet it has impressed itself so firmly upon his consciousness he cannot take his eyes off it. It is incredible, but if he is thinking anything of Jesus at all it is probably as someone who might be able to help him into the water. If this were a movie with a hero the audience would be yelling from their seats, "Forget the pool, turn around, turn around. Look at Jesus. He's your healer, not the water."

There is a very subtle trap we must be careful to avoid if our faith is to remain centered in God - we must not let the miracle become the object of our attention. Waiting for the waters to stir, Poolside is looking for a certain effect rather than looking to the 'Effecter'. The Deliverer - not the miracle - must remain the center of our focus. The reason for that is very obvious. Miracles usually come in ways we haven't expected. It would be the testimony of a great many

Christians that God's answer to a specific prayer came in ways they never anticipated. God will make a way where there appears to be no way. How He will do so, though, we have no idea. But because Poolside is locked in to the notion his healing will come about through the bubbling waters of the pool he is not open to other possibilities. So he sits and waits, and waits. For thirty eight years he waits.

I want to contrast Poolside with another person whom we shall call Rooftop. Like Poolside he is paralyzed laying on a pallet unable to walk. He too is hoping for a miracle. However, there the similarities end. Rooftop is a far more resourceful and determined person and unlike Poolside, Rooftop has his eyes fixed firmly upon Jesus. Borne along on his pallet by some friends he arrives at the building where Jesus is inside teaching and healing people. Unable to get in because of the crowd, his friends carry Rooftop onto the roof and pulling away the tiles, they let the paralyzed man down through the roof right in front of Jesus. Now that's 'in - your - face' faith. Perhaps too audacious for some people, but not too outrageous for Jesus, who commended the men for their faith.

Rooftop and Poolside, two paralyzed men lying helplessly on a pallet. One found a way to get near to Jesus under daunting circumstances, the other saw himself as a victim of circumstances and when he did get alongside Jesus had only his tale of woe. Before going on I need to make clear I am not contrasting action with waiting, and concluding a person of faith is always a man of action. Nor am I implying a person who has waited a long time for their hope has no faith. That is not the distinction I want to draw. The difference between these two men can be summed up in one word, passivity. Poolside has come to terms with his condition and is too acquiescent. He has none of the

Poolside and Rooftop

resourcefulness and determination of Rooftop. The lack of these qualities is evidence of a lack of faith.

For those of us who have an unfulfilled hope and have been lying languidly on our pallet too long, the question we must ask ourselves is the same one Jesus posed to Poolside; "Do you (really) want to get healed?" "Yes but someone always gets in the water before me," he replies. There is a 'but' in his life. You have to get rid of the 'but' - it's an excuse for failure. Whenever a 'but' qualifies our 'yes' it means we are simply not sufficiently motivated. "Sure I want to improve my marriage, but my husband (wife) won't take time to go to counseling." "Sure I want to further my career but I get overlooked for promotions." "Yes I would like to make a career change and go to back to college but I can't afford it. I have a family I'm responsible for." But, but, but. 'But' is evidence the desire in a person is not very strong and easily thwarted.

When we read Rooftop's story in the Gospel of Luke, chapter five, we see that before he went up onto the roof he and his friends tried to get to Jesus through the door but were prevented from doing so by the crowd. There was the opportunity for a 'but' had he and his friends so chosen. "Well, we tried," they could have told their families later, "but the crowd was so thick around the house it was impossible to get anywhere within fifty feet of Jesus." The opportunity was there for an excuse if they had been less resolute. Because their desire was so strong, immediately seeing one way blocked Rooftop and his companions cast about for another way to get to Jesus. When someone truly desires something there always is another way - though maybe not an obvious one. An old adage says "Love finds a way." I guarantee that when there's a sigh in your heart and there seems to be nothing left to do, there is always one more step you can take. Opportunities are found by those who are looking. Whether you find a means to press forward or see the way ahead blocked, depends ultimately on the intensity of your desire.

There are always plenty of people ready to tell us something cannot be done. Probably many people in the crowd that day told Rooftop and his friends as they tried to push past, "There's no way you can get inside that house." However, these nay sayers had no desire to get in the house themselves. Without motivation they judged only by appearances and missed the potential for creative possibilities uncovered by Rooftop and his friends.

As Christians we have taught and emphasized that faith waits patiently for the promises of God. Maybe we have forgotten, or never realized, that faith also acts with resourcefulness. I once read that a genius is defined as someone who creates opportunities for themself. Rooftop created his opportunity and was commended by Jesus for his faith. I've often heard the comment, "We've prayed about it and left it in God's hands." It may be, as far as God is concerned, that He's left it in your hands.

It was a particular experience in my own life that shaped my observations regarding Poolside and Rooftop. The ordeal taught me not to ignore the sigh if I want to be an overcomer in life. The involuntary groan which swells up from some deep recesses within our being is an indication the forces being brought to bear upon our life are shaping it in such a way as to exclude hope.

In all the time we were waiting to go to America we hadn't heard even once directly from the ministry. Our invitation to be part of the school came through another party. Progress reports of preparations to begin the school came indirectly, usually through newsletters. I began to feel it was taking too long. I confided my restlessness to

Poolside and Rooftop 73

Jan and we began to pray about it. An acquaintance suggested we write to the ministry, but since they knew of our desire to come, I questioned whether anything was to be gained by my writing. Actually I was worried they might see it as impatience and lack of faith on my part. A day or two later Jan picked up on this person's comments and suggested we contact them and see what was happening. Again I downplayed the suggestion, "No, we have to wait for them to get ready. Then they will write us with the dates of the school and we can go."

The trouble was I couldn't get rid of the sigh, I just did not have peace about doing nothing. It was a dilemma. Then a few days later Jan said, "You know, I wouldn't just give up this venture without a fight. I would write." Until that point I hadn't seen writing the letter in terms of fighting for something we believed in. When she put it that way, for the first time I saw writing the letter from a different perspective, as an aggressive act of faith, rather than a tentative note of inquiry.

Like poolside who was looking to the pool for his healing, I was looking for the letter that never came. My whole life revolved around that letter. When I woke up the first thing I thought of was that maybe today the letter would come. During the day the thought helped pass the time in an uninteresting job. And after work I hurried home to see whether it had come. I was relying upon people I did not know to make my dreams come true.

I had a goal and a plan to accomplish that goal. I assumed that by sticking to my plan I was demonstrating faith. I would have described my faith as single minded, but in truth I was narrow minded. Now while it is good to have a plan, a narrow minded person believes there is only one way to accomplish the goal - their plan. Narrow minded faith digs in and sees advice not in line with their strategy as an attempt to sway them from course. I was so sure the act of faith called for me to do nothing but wait for the letter that I wouldn't consider alternative suggestions. I was so wrong. James 3:17 says the wisdom from above is reasonable - that is to say, it is amenable to other views and willing to yield. I learned from experience that staying open and receptive to other ideas is an essential element of faith.

So I wrote the letter of inquiry. Then I waited. When a suitable time had passed and there was no response I sent another letter. Still no response. So I sent a telegram. Finally a reply came back from one of the elders in the community who said the founder was away on a ministry trip, but when he returned they would be making some decisions concerning the school. Finally, after a long delay we received a letter ... "Unable to make progress due to finances ...on indefinite hold until the Lord should provide sufficient funds to complete the building... appreciate your interest, keep in touch."

Oh, how my spirit sank when I read that letter. After waiting so long it felt like a physical blow. *Keep in touch!* Those words seemed so uncaring, almost dismissive. I asked myself, "What do I do in the meantime, get another job and hang out until we hear from them again, if we ever do?" Frankly I had had it with low-paying part-time menial jobs. The thought of getting another one for some indeterminate time didn't excite me one bit. All I wanted was to get on with God's plan for my life. It seemed fulfilling our destiny was on hold due to an uncompleted building somewhere in Northern Minnesota.

I was down in spirits for a day or so. Then as I was pondering developments all of a sudden the following thought just popped into my consciousness, "Have you considered that the sigh in your heart is the way I feel

Poolside and Rooftop

too?" It was such a novel thought it startled me. "Was that God?" I asked myself. Did He feel the same way about the delay that I did? Was it also God's wish these people get the school up and running without delay? What if my heavy feelings in response to the letter were not born of impatience? What if the sigh in my heart was the Holy Spirit? Was my heart really beating in time with God's? Were He and I of one mind in this matter? The more I thought about it the more the Holy Spirit quickened my spirit that I was right and I should act on this basis. It was a defining moment in our quest to go to America. Instead of passively accepting the status quo as the will of God and falling in with it, I decided to challenge the ministry in their decision.

I wrote a letter. It was a good letter - better than good, it was a Holy Ghost letter. It was forceful and unequivocal without being rude. I spoke my mind and the words when I read them through later exactly replicated my thoughts and convictions. I told Jan, "That is how I feel. Either it will get us in or it will get us rejected altogether." Among the things I pointed out was that there were other people besides themselves involved whose lives were on hold while they delayed starting the school. If they appreciated how eager we were to come and how much it meant to us, they never could have taken such a casual, lackadaisical attitude to the delay. I pointed out that a school was not a building; a school consisted of teachers and students. We have both parties present, yourselves as teachers and us, the students. So what stops you from beginning now?

You might call it 'in - your - face' faith. I'll tell you how I'm thinking. The same way as the Gentile woman who confronted Jesus and boldly argued her case persuading Jesus to grant her desire (Mathew 15:27). Jesus was going to refuse her request until she persuaded him she should not be overlooked. He admired her spunk. Well I had a case too, and so far as I was concerned I felt it was legitimate.

I mailed the letter and waited. You know what happened? Nothing! No reply. I gave it a month and not having heard I decided to find their number and call on the phone. Do you know how I was feeling? Let me tell you. The same way as Rooftop; Jesus is in that house and by hook or by crook Rooftop is going to get an audience with Jesus. He says to himself "I want to be healed and the man who can heal me is right at hand. I need to get near Him. Now is the time, I need to seize this opportunity." Now Jesus may reject him, but one thing Jesus will not be able to do is ignore him. Rooftop could wait; what is one more hour, another two. But this man has waited too long already. It's time. Nothing is to be gained by waiting, only a chance that everything may be lost. This is the last push to the summit of a very determined man who, looking at the crowd stopping him, says, "Look out I'm coming through, you are in my way."

So I made the call. I will never forget the elation of that moment, hearing on the phone a voice with an American accent saying our perseverance had paid off. We were to make our arrangements to come. They had reconsidered as a result of my communication and decided to go ahead and start the school!

I learned from that experience. It was a defining moment in my faith. Be guided by your heart in matters of faith. We forget too easily we have an enemy. For us to get our way means the devil suffers loss. Satan is cunning and will use any means, even fellow Christians to obstruct us. Don't take 'no' for an answer unless you are sure it comes from God. Too often we are passive and tentative when we should be forceful and assertive. We accept our lot in life without

Poolside and Rooftop

demur when circumstances conspire to exclude a meaningful future. It is not wrong to be insistent and plead our case when our hopes are thwarted. God admires those who will press in and won't be easily fobbed off, people like Rooftop and the gentile woman who argued with Jesus and got her wish.

When we arrived finally in December of 1983 in Northern Minnesota a number of people upon meeting us for the first time told us how it was my letter that got the school going. One person told me they remembered exactly the day my letter came, and they recounted, "I will never forget Art coming out of his trailer excitedly waving the letter in his hand after reading it." It is a heady feeling, a good feeling, an exciting feeling to know your actions have advanced God's agenda. More than that it is a great confidence booster for following the leading of the holy Spirit. I went with my gut feeling, and what I sensed in my spirit was the witness of the Holy Spirit.

At one of the early school sessions Art said he had a shoebox full of applications for the school. I looked around the room at the seven of us from different parts of the world who were in the class. Just seven. I wondered what happened to those others who, like us, felt led of God to come to this school yet never made it.

I taught my boys to swim by coaxing them to jump into the swimming pool where I waited to catch them. Standing at the edge of the pool they looked at me, looked at the water, and shook their heads. They believed in me, and did not doubt I would not let them come to harm. Still it was not enough to get them to jump. This shows us that faith is not just a matter of believing, it is also a matter of trust. Trusting God is the hardest part of faith. Many of us can believe in God, but making ourselves vulnerable and trusting He will save us is another matter altogether.

If you are serious about doing the will of God, sooner or later you will find yourself standing on the side of the pool looking down into the water. There always comes an action part of faith. A moment when we must step out in obedience to God's leading. Faith involves risk. If your faith has not required you to take chances, then you have not been fully living the faith.

Faith Involves Risk

chapter six

I had imagined this moment innumerable times the past two years. In the morning when I woke, and at night when I went to sleep it was the first and last thought on my mind. By day my reveries helped pass the time in a succession of boring jobs as I waited what seemed like forever. Now we were living the dream, we had boarded the plane on the first leg of our flight to Hawaii, Los Angeles and then on to our final destination, a small obscure Christian community in northern Minnesota named Ben Israel Ministries.

We had little idea what lay ahead. We knew almost nothing about the ministry or what to expect beyond the fact that there would be a school of sorts which we would attend as founding students along with some others from Africa and Europe. We had looked forward to this moment ever since God had shown us we were to go there for a 'time of learning and preparation'. God's call not only gave us the direction we sought at the time, it created a hope that grew and grew into an overwhelming desire. For the last two years nothing else mattered for us except attending this Bible school. At times when it seemed unlikely the school would even get started due to lack of funds and resources, I would doubt and question whether we really had heard from God. Was this just a flame of my own kindling? Maybe I would wake up tomorrow and come to my senses. When time would go by with no word from the ministry, Jan and I would sometimes go out to dinner at Auckland International Airport and watch planes take off, anticipating the day we would make our own departure. The hope of going to Ben Israel never did go away, not even at those times when everything seemed against it. Hope brought us back to the airport restaurant to bolster our faith, and each trip to the airport fanned the flames of our desire to be on a plane and going to America. Now it was a reality.

We had said all our good-byes and were seated in the plane awaiting takeoff, my first trip overseas, only Jan's second. We were airborne at last and a feeling of apprehension intruded on my excitement; we didn't have a return ticket. Not only did we not have a return ticket, we did not have enough money to support ourselves for a year's stay in America. Once we got to Los Angeles and bought our ticket to Minnesota we would have less than two hundred dollars. Flying high over the Pacific the consulate official's words come back to me; "A visa does not guarantee you the right of entry into the United States. That decision rests with the officer at the port of entry. A visa only allows you to present yourself and seek entry." The trouble was our Bible school was not an officially recognized school, it had no official status. This had caused problems when we applied for our visa, but eventually the consulate issued us a special visa for a year's stay. That visa, it seemed, was only good provided the officer at the point of entry was satisfied. What if he wasn't convinced

Faith Involves Risk

the school existed or qualified as a bone fide school? What if he questioned us and found out how little money we had, or that we did not have a return ticket? He wouldn't allow us entry, that's what would happen.

It had been a dilemma for us when we finally were told by Ben Israel Ministries that the school would be starting and we could be in it. We didn't have enough money to make the trip. What should we do? Turn down the opportunity? This is what we had devoted the last two years of our life to. It was I who had pushed Ben Israel to start this school when they were ready to put it on indefinite hold. Now that it was finally coming off should we beg off for lack of finances? All the time we waited for the go ahead to make the trip we had been saving every penny we could toward our fare and expenses. But the economy was not good and the jobs we got were for the most part temporary and poorly paid. It seemed no sooner did we get some money together than we lost our job and such savings as we had put away were used up to tide us over to the next job. This pattern of being in and out of work seemed to continue all the time until we finally got the O.K. to make our arrangements to go to Ben Israel. When we added up our pennies there was not enough.

Jan and I couldn't bear the thought of waiting any longer, we agreed we should proceed. We had come this far, we would give it our best shot. If God was in this venture, somehow He would bring it about. If we failed we did not want it to be for lack of trust or effort on our part. We would take it as far as we could until either God opened the door or it shut firmly. In these situations you take it step by step, and the first step was to find out how far we could get with the money we had. So we called a travel agent and found out that if we got a one way ticket to Los Angeles we should have enough left to get a one way ticket to Minnesota and there would be some - but not much - left over. People knowledgeable about overseas travel told us you had to have a return ticket to travel overseas. We decided if the travel agent had no qualms about selling us a one way ticket, then we would take the next step and apply for a visa at the American consulate. The travel agent was willing to sell us a one way ticket, and even booked us on a flight. We said we didn't have a visa yet and she said it was no problem, we needn't pay until you we got our visa and if it didn't come in time she would simply rebook us on a later flight.

So off it was to the American consulate where we told the official we wanted to go to the United States for a year and attend a Christian school. Thus began a series of visits to the consulate to satisfy all their requirements, a process that took many weeks and required us to revisit the travel agent several times and rebook our flight as each departure date came and went. All the time I expected that sooner or later amongst the forms I had to fill out would be some question requiring us to declare we had a return ticket and sufficient finances for a year's stay. Then it would all be over. We would have taken it as far as we could, or perhaps at the last minute God would miraculously provide the extra money we needed.

We prayed as fervently as we could. To lose out at this late stage would have been hard. We wondered how God would provide, but nothing happened - no mysterious stranger came up and said, 'God has told me I am to give you this sum of money.' To my constant surprise as our visa application progressed and went through all the red tape, the consulate never inquired about our ticket arrangements, nor asked us any questions regarding how we were financing our stay overseas. And so without telling a lie or misleading anyone in any way the day finally came

Faith Involves Risk

when we had satisfied all visa requirements and with visa in hand were able to go and purchase our ticket. Now we were on a plane bound for the USA, and for the first time in two years I was apprehensive.

In any major undertaking there comes a moment when you realize that if you are to proceed further you are totally committed. You cannot go back. At least not without great loss. Up until this juncture all discussion and planning is driven by the thought of reward. At the point of committal any attendant risks, which until then have remained in the background, assume a significance and weightiness that overshadows the prize. It is at the point of committal, poised between the past and the future, when we are most vulnerable to fear. If we lack courage this is when we are most likely to back down.

As the children of Israel wandered in the wilderness they were poised between the past and the future. The slavery and oppression of Egypt lay behind them, the Promised land lay ahead. This nomadic tribe was about to become a nation and fulfill the promise God made to their forefather, Abraham hundreds of years earlier, "To your descendants I will give this land" (Genesis 12:7). 'A land flowing with milk and honey' was how God described this fertile and productive land. The climate was such that rain would water their crops. They wouldn't have the hard labor of bringing water up from the Nile for irrigation as in Egypt. Most wonderful of all, the produce of their labors belonged to them, not a tyrannical overlord. 'The Promised Land!' How that phrase must have quickened many a weary son of Israel as they journeyed in the wilderness. Now God's chosen people stood poised to go in and take the promised land, and fulfill the destiny God had in liberating them from Egypt. Chapters 13 and 14 of Numbers tell the story of what happened when they reached the borders of the promised land. Spies returning from spying out the land reported that indeed it was a rich and bountiful land, but there were also strong inhabitants who dwelt there in fortified cities. After discussing the report the Israelites decided not to go in and take the promised land, "for they are too strong for us." At the very moment Israel was about to realize it's objective they froze with fear.

All the time the Israelites were in the wilderness they had anticipated the day when they would settle in the promised land, raise their own crops and enjoy the fruit of their labors. Arriving at the border they saw the enemy for the first time. And the enemy was big. "We're all going to die. What have we done? Oh we should have stayed in Egypt". Out of fear the Israelites abandoned the dream when it was within reach in favor of returning to the misery of Egypt they had left behind. The goal of fear is to make a person panic and draw back. The dynamics of fear are universal - make the victim underestimate their own power while overestimating that of the adversary. The threat is held over the victim causing them to question their ability to succeed, and let up and change course. When Israel saw the enemy they saw themselves as grasshoppers. This is what happens when you contemplate obstacles, you become demoralized. Israel saw themselves as puny and no match for the enemy. They completely forgot the one thing they had going for them, God, whose saving presence in the wilderness had kept them.

Sitting in a plane thousands of feet above the Pacific I contemplated the obstacles that lay ahead. The enormity of what we were attempting hit me - trying to get into the USA on a one way ticket and stay a year with barely enough money to last a month. My resolve wavered. Our quest suddenly seemed a foolhardy venture. "We won't get past

Faith Involves Risk

immigration. We should have waited and saved up more money," I told myself. I was convinced we would be refused entry and put on the next plane back to New Zealand.

Fear feeds on itself and before long escalates into a worse case scenario. "Even if I do get through customs," I asked myself, "how will they respond at the ministry when we arrive with not enough money for our support?" True, they hadn't stipulated any fees or stated any amount we should bring by way of costs but I didn't expect a free ride. We are going to arrive with almost no money. What was I thinking? I wasn't thinking!

How do you stand firm when every instinct is to turn on your heels and run? For the answer to that question we have the example of Caleb and Joshua. Of the ten spies who went into the land only Caleb and Joshua were for going on. They exhorted the congregation of the sons of Israel, saying, *"The land which we passed through to spy out is an exceedingly good land. If the LORD is pleased with us, then He will bring us into this land, and give it to us - a land which flows with milk and honey. Only do not rebel against the LORD; and do not fear the people of the land, for they shall be our prey. Their protection has been removed from them, and the LORD is with us; do not fear them"* (Numbers 14:7 - 9). Caleb and Joshua didn't try to minimize the danger. They knew they were up against it, but they didn't falter. Yes the enemy is big, they admitted, but God is with us. The opposition is real, the threat is real enough, but so is God. God is real too and God is on the side of Israel. He is more than a match for any obstacle.

The key to courage is the knowledge and confidence that God is with you. There is no need to exaggerate your own capabilities. You do not have to thump your chest and do a war dance as native tribes once did to work themselves up into a frenzy before going in to battle. Caleb and Joshua saw the enemy, but they saw something else. They saw that God was on their side, and beholding God they saw themselves as unbeatable. With God on our side we are more than a match for any adversary. Whatever we are up against, God is more than able. We have already seen that when David went up against Goliath, he was not intimidated by his size. David saw only one thing, an arrogant boastful man who came against God. David's boldness was not bravado, it was a firm confidence based entirely on the conviction that God was on his side. Only those who are confidant in their relationship with God and His calling will stand firm - *"but the people who know their God will display strength and take action" (Daniel 11:32).*

Flying above the Pacific I reflected on the circumstances behind our quest to go to America, our goal the past several years. Did we have to go overseas to serve God? Couldn't we do it in New Zealand we were asked? Why America? Because that is where God had shown us we were to go. This is what I kept coming back to on the plane, the conviction that God was sending us and if this trip were His doing He would be with us. Of course people can be wrong about hearing God. Were we wrong? All I could say to that is I believed I had heard God. Jan believed it too, so we were in agreement, an important consideration in any faith venture. And for over two years we had thought of nothing else.

I remember when I worked at an animal feeds factory, there was a library across the road and I used to go over there and look at the atlas they had because it was huge, the only one I had seen with enough detail to list the postal address of the ministry we were going to. Laporte, was the name of the little town. I went home and told Jan excitedly, "I found out where we are going. I saw it on a map." I made many trips to that library in my lunch hour and would peer at it to get an idea of the country where we were going, of which I knew nothing. I noticed numerous lakes. I remember particularly seeing these two huge lakes not too far from where we would be, Upper Red Lake and Lower Red Lake. I found a book too that had this to say about a town not too far from our destination, 'International Falls, the ice box of America, where national temperatures are typically the lowest.' So it snowed and was cold in Minnesota. Sitting on the plane I drew comfort from these thoughts. Surely such a desire sustained for over two years with the odds so stacked against it could not be a romantic notion - it could only be the working of the Holy Spirit leading me in the knowledge of God's will.

Surely God was with us. The clincher was a little episode that happened when we first applied at the American consulate for a visa. The official was unhelpful to the point of rudeness when I approached him at his station for a visa. He wouldn't answer any of my questions as to what visa I should apply for and how to proceed. "What visa are you applying for?" he interrupted me rudely as I solicited information.

"I am not sure what category I should apply under," I replied. "Here is what I want to do ..."

"I am not here to teach you how to apply for a visa," he interrupted curtly.

For about a minute it went back and forth as I tried to get information from a totally unresponsive and uncaring official. He was talking loudly and I felt every eye in the room was watching, engrossed in the drama. I was at a loss how to proceed. Jan told me later she was praying rapidly. I did too, "Lord this man is not being helpful. Make him help us." The transformation was immediate.

"You need to ask me this question," he said, startling me with the change in his manner.

So I asked him and he told me the answer. "Now you need to ask me this," he said. And so it went on with him leading me through all the questions until I had all the information I needed and made my application. As we concluded he told me, "Now, this will take some time, you will need to come back again as this application proceeds. When you do ask for me, here is my card." And he handed me his card. Throughout the whole process of application which took some weeks we dealt with this official who went out of his way to facilitate our visa application. That was God.

Going in at the flood.

As the second generation of Israel made preparations under Joshua to enter the promised land, God instructed them, *"Every place on which the sole of your foot treads I have given it to You ... only be strong and very courageous" (Joshua 1:3,7).* God speaks as if the conquest is an accomplished fact, yet at the same time exhorts them to be brave. Our destiny is tied directly to our courage. Apart from Caleb and Joshua, the generation of Israelites who left Egypt all perished in the wilderness because they were afraid. They never saw the promised land - a sobering reminder that Gods plan and intentions for our life can be thwarted if we lack courage.

There is an interesting phrase, which a casual reader might easily miss, in the biblical record of the Israelites preparations to cross the Jordan. The record notes the Jordan was flooding it's banks! In other words it was the most inopportune time they could have chosen to cross the river. An already hazardous venture was exacerbated by going in at the flood. The Israelites might lose men and weapons on the crossing, and if that didn't happen the inhabitants of the land might attack before the full company had crossed and were at full strength. With nowhere to retreat they would be wiped out. The potential existed for a disaster.

At the point of committal there is a river flooding it's banks, some hazard that increases the risk. If you let it unnerve you and force you to turn back, you jeopardize your destiny in God. There is no such thing as faith without risk. In any faith endeavor there exists the possibility for failure. Even with the most careful planning there will always be some attendant risk due to circumstances outside your control. Foresight is no match for hindsight; you cannot remove the element of risk in life. Men and women of faith do not wait until all opposition is removed. They press on, confidant God will take care of their adversary and bring them safely into the land of promise.

Entry into the USA.

The moment finally arrives and Jan and I are standing in the customs hall at Hawaii airport, a huge room with rows and rows of passengers lined up waiting their turn to clear immigration. It was only 6 or 7am and even at that early hour very humid . Jan and I stood at the back of the hall for a while. I was trying to make up my mind which line to join. Looking at the faces of the officials, I sought one who wasn't questioning people too closely, preferably someone with his mind only half on his job who would just stamp our passport disinterestedly and allow us to pass through unchallenged. Eventually I made up my mind and we joined the tail end of one line. When it came our turn at the counter he looked at our visa carefully, saw that it was for a year, noting the purpose of our trip which was set forth on a separate paper the US consulate had given us. It stated the name of the religious organization we were to stay with and the fact that our trip was for educational purpose of attending a school. Immediately he began questioning us closely about the school; "What sort of school is it?" he asked, and then consulting some hidden book out of my sight added, "they are not listed as an official school." The truth was I had no idea what sort of school it was. In their newsletter Ben Israel ministries called it a prophetic school, that was as much as I knew. How do you tell a secular official, "This is a prophetic school, sir." What is a prophetic school? I barely had any idea myself. I tried to explain as best I could that it was a Christian ministry which was only for the first time venturing into a new dimension of ministry by starting this school. "What is the curriculum?" he asked. Again I had no idea. So far as I knew they didn't even have a school building, much less a curriculum. My hesitant replies only made him more antagonistic.

"Was this a Jewish organization?" he asked in reference to the name Ben Israel Ministries.

"How many people live there?"

"How many members are Jewish?"

I had no idea of the answers to any of these questions and my unhelpful replies were provoking his annoyance. The situation was rapidly deteriorating and my worst fears on the plane were being realized. My answers were not satisfying his curiosity and he found my ignorance suspicious. I guess he suspected me of being deliberately uncooperative, or hiding something. He was alternately asking me questions and then consulting some reference book out of sight. Jan was standing silently by my side. I looked about the customs hall which a little earlier had been full of people to find that Jan and I and one or two stragglers were the only ones left.

Then he asked me one of the two questions I was dreading, "How much money do you have with you?" "Here goes," I thought to myself, "once he knows how little we have he will want to see our tickets. When he sees we only have a one way ticket his suspicious mind will immediately jump to the conclusion we plan on remaining in the country as illegal immigrants." It would be all over before it even began. Heart in mouth I told him how much we had. Incredibly he did not hear my reply. At the very moment I opened my mouth and spoke another official interrupted him and the two left to confer a little distance away.

I knew he would return in a moment or two and repeat his question. I began to pray while I awaited the official's return. "Lord" I said, "everyone else has passed through customs except us. And of everyone on the plane we more than anyone have a right to pass into the country because you have called us here. It is not right that we should be refused entry. We do not intend any wrong during our stay. In no way do we pose any sort of threat to the country. We are coming for legitimate and honorable reasons. We intend to leave again. We are not going to break any laws. America does not have any cause to be concerned about us. My Father, you have sent us here, but this man is opposing your will. Unless you intervene here and make a way for us to enter we will very likely be sent back to New Zealand."

The customs officer finished his conversation with the other official and returned to his desk. Whether they had been talking about us or some unrelated matter I had no idea. Fully expecting him to continue questioning us where he left off, I steeled myself for the question to be repeated. Instead he stamped our passports lying on the desk and without any further questions or comment we were through. A hostile and suspicious customs officer for no reason that we could see waived his suspicions and simply allowed us to enter the USA. His action was an abrupt and complete about face, the same as we had experienced with the American consular official when we first applied for our visa. God is so great. We were walking on air, unable to believe we were in the USA. And what a last hurdle it had been. Outside the airport on the sidewalk I looked around. This was America. We made it. We made it! It felt good, real good.

In trying to uncover and follow God's will in my life I feel at times as if I am walking toward a person I can barely see in the distance. Drawn by an irresistible desire to reach Him I am hindered by many obstacles that lie along the way. In following hard after God it is as if I am walking across the fields toward Him and always there is one more fence in the way, one more ditch to get by. I manage somehow and continue toward Him. And I keep coming, but He remains tantalizingly yonder. I wonder why he doesn't do more to help me. Only through sheer persistence on my part do I make any progress. I sense I am being watched but He does nothing to encourage me. He just watches and observes. I feel at times as if I am forcing my way into God's kingdom without His help. Sitting in the meadow contemplating yet another high fence blocking the way, you question whether God is really for you. Am I wanted, am I really called of God? Did I really hear Him tell me to go to the USA? Why don't you help us Lord? There are times you get discouraged. So when it looks for all the world as if the last fence in the form of a hostile customs officer will be too much for us - and in a moment (literally) that fence is supernaturally removed.... oh, what it does for your faith! But more, much more than that, is the wonderful confirmation and reassurance that God is with us in this venture. "My presence shall go with you," God assured Moses. God is with us. I wanted to shout it out loud. It was as if God had drawn up close beside Jan and me, put His arm around us in our moment of entry into the promised land and said, "You know I am with you. I am for you. You know that don't you? I am going to use you greatly. You are going to do things for me you have never imagined. I am going to take you to places you have never been." And it makes me want to cry because I want so much to be used of God.

Jesus is watching us. From a distance. We think we are alone, making it as best we can, but we are not alone. We are being observed by One who is waiting for us, who has always been watching over our life, waiting for us to arrive.

Increase Our Faith

chapter seven

And when the disciples saw Him (Jesus) walking on the sea, they were frightened, saying, "It is a ghost!" And they cried out for fear. But immediately Jesus spoke to them, saying, "Take courage, it is I; do not be afraid." And Peter answered Him and said, "Lord, if it is You, command me to come to You on the water." And He said, "Come!" And Peter got out of the boat, and walked on the water and came toward Jesus.
(Matthew 14:26 - 29)

Impetuosity or spontaneity?

If Peter were alive today he would be a poster boy for Nike. Their 'Just do it' motto characterized Peter's approach to faith. His response to seeing Jesus walking on water was to call out, *"Lord, if it is You, command me to come to You on the water."* We all know Peter took his eyes off Jesus and sank. Most Bible scholars have concluded this was a failure, a hasty and ill advised act on Peter's part in committing himself beyond what he was able to achieve.

The almost universal consensus of opinion is that Peter was impetuous and this character flaw lay behind Peter's reckless action. I want to challenge this traditional censorious characterization of Peter.

Peter's response in getting out of the boat to walk on water toward Jesus was not an impetuous act, it was a spontaneous reaction. Impetuosity or spontaneity, what's the difference? There is a difference - a big difference. Enough at least to turn a defect of character into a virtue and force a re-evaluation of this incident. Because Peter was apt to speak and act without thinking and frequently over-reached himself, it is generally assumed he was impetuous. The dictionary defines 'impetuosity' as an unplanned sudden action stemming from an unruly and undisciplined impulse. The necessary qualities of self control and restraint are lacking in the character of impetuous people. Spontaneity is also an unpremeditated action, but there is one important difference; instead of being violent and headstrong, spontaneity is an instinctive involuntary response natural and unaffected, due to the harmony (or disharmony) of the mix and match of the elements combined. For instance if you rub two pieces of wood together rapidly you get spontaneous combustion.

When we look at this incident keep in mind Peter is a disciple. The word means 'follower.' The relationship between these two men is more than that of student and teacher: a disciple is an adherent whose heart has been captivated by the one he follows. It is implicitly understood between master and disciple that all the master's actions are a model to be imitated by the disciple. Nothing is more natural than for Peter the disciple to follow Jesus' example. When Peter sees Jesus on the water he is drawn to emulate Him by an impulse he cannot resist. The disciples saw Jesus coming across the water and they were afraid,

Increase Our Faith

thinking they had seen a ghost. Once the Lord revealed Himself, Peter, the first to recover said "Lord, if it is you bid me come." Those words are consistent with the relationship that existed between the two men, that of disciple and teacher. Peter's actions were in keeping with those of a disciple. Had Peter attempted the feat of walking on water without asking Jesus permission it might fairly be called impetuous. He didn't. He sought Jesus' consent in a spontaneous reaction to seeing Jesus walk on the water.

Peter understood that Jesus deeds were an example to be emulated, as Jesus Himself made clear to His disciples on the eve of His crucifixion; *"Truly, truly, I say to you, he who believes in Me, the works that I do shall he do also; and greater works than these shall he do; because I go to the Father" (John 14:12).* Those who rush to condemn Peter's action as hasty should not overlook one very important fact, the Lord was pleased at Peter's request to walk on the waves and encouraged his fledgling faith. Christ bid Peter come. Not in order to show him up. Nor for the thrill of the experience. He called Peter to Him across the water so that he would know and experience His power. Jesus wants us to know the power of God that can be released in response to faith.

For a while Peter was walking on water, something no man has done before or since. This was a remarkable feat, hardly a failure. Commentators have placed too much emphasis on Peter sinking and not nearly enough on his act of walking on water. In so doing they have turned an accomplishment into a failure. Faith is learned just like any discipline in life is learned, by watching and copying. We are bound to make mistakes. What is worse, to fail like Peter by over reaching, or remain in the boat and risk being the cautious failure? Yes, we might find ourselves sinking beneath the waves, we probably will mess up at times, but the Lord's hand is not too short to save. If we stay in the boat we will never make a fool of our selves - but neither will we experience the power of God that can be released in response to faith.

A man I knew who attended church made the remark, "It may be in the Bible, but I've never seen it in the church." It was a dismissive remark expressing the thought that things in the Bible outside his realm of experience had little relevance to his life. In his opinion, attention and consideration of such matters was not compelling. This comment has always stayed with me as a statement of unbelief. His indifference toward spiritual matters makes me question the fervency of his love for Christ. This man's singular lack of curiosity is hardly demonstrative of a follower.

The unexamined faith can never do the works of God that bring eternal reward. The untested faith can never realize God's purpose in our life. Peter saw Jesus walk on water and immediately said "Lord if it is you bid me come." These are the true sentiments of a disciple. This is the passionate plea of disciples whose heart has been captured and will do anything to follow the one they love.

"Increase our faith!"

The true disciple can never be content in the role of a passive onlooker. You cannot sit in a pew taking in the word of God Sunday after Sunday and not be moved by the possibilities of faith. As the disciples followed Jesus they saw Him doing things no man had ever done, and like true disciples they said to the Lord, "Increase our faith!" And the Lord said, *"If you had faith like a mustard seed, you would say to this mulberry tree, 'Be uprooted and be planted in the sea'; and it would obey you" (Luke 17:6).* Jesus responds to their request by pointing out the possibilities of faith. Notice he doesn't tell them how to have more faith. He does not give them a course to gradually increase their faith. There is not a five step program to a bigger faith. No, He stirs their imagination by pointing to the possibilities of faith, and they are staggering. Who has seen a mulberry tree uprooted and planted in the sea? Such a deed lies outside our realm of experience. An unbeliever says, "You can sit and pray all day for that mulberry tree to be planted in the sea and it will never happen." Jesus tells us if we have the faith, God will do it. In effect Jesus is saying, "When it comes to faith I want you to think big. I'm not going to tie your hands. I am not going to limit you." The message is this: you've no idea what you can do with faith. Get out there and have a go.

Have you ever noticed the almost reckless way Jesus talks about faith? "Whatever you ask and believe you shall receive." And again in another instance He tells the disciples, "and nothing shall be impossible to you." You will note Jesus doesn't qualify faith as we do. There are no limits. "Ask anything you want, I will give you," and again, "Whatever two or three of you agree in my name I will grant you." By comparison we so often say "God can move the Mulberry tree, *if it is His will.*" We tack "if it is His will" on the end because we want to protect someone against the disappointment of unanswered prayer. Jesus is less concerned about presumptive prayer, than the likelihood of our not asking enough.

As we commit to following Christ we find ourselves being led down paths we had not foreseen that require a radical trust and commitment. God does not show us more than He deems it necessary for us to know. He does not take us into His counsel concerning His purposes for our life like some field marshal conferring with his generals about his strategy to fight the enemy on the eve of a battle.

So Jan and I like others led of God found ourselves without a home and leaving our job to wait on Him for direction. "Was this really the Lord's leading?" we asked ourselves, and like Peter we could only say, "Lord if this is you, bid us come," adding at the same time, "Lord increase our faith." Then later we had our direction and the invitation to go to the USA, but not enough money. Do we go? Is it prudent? Is this God's leading or not? Again prayerfully we said, "Lord if this is you bid us come." And so we found ourselves on a plane going to the USA with a one way ticket, whispering under our breath, "Lord increase our faith."

We have taken chances perhaps others might think risky. Yet I do not think I am any less prudent and careful than the next man. The fact of the matter is I want more than anything to know and follow God's plan for my life. The times I've taken a risk is when I felt I had no option, for to do nothing would have been to fail to act on the leading of God. Given Jesus' words concerning the mulberry tree I do not think we have any choice when God leads but to be willing to put ourselves in a position whereby if God does not come through for us, we fail. Jan and I said at the outset when we made our decision to leave our job to find God's will, "We will take this as far as we can. We will follow God's leading as we understand it, until it leads somewhere or comes to nothing. But let's go for broke, let's not hold back. If God has called us, somehow He will provide for us and make His will clear." We were young in the Lord, naive in matters of faith when we uttered those words but I have never had cause to regret them. Looking back now in hindsight I might do some things differently if I were placed in the same situations. But so far as my philosophy is concerned it is essentially the same: there is only one way to follow the Lord - go for broke. Just do it. I believe this with all my heart. I believed it as a young believer. I believe it today nearly twenty years later. It is better to make a mistake trying, than let God down by not giving Him the opportunity to move the mulberry tree.

Don't be a cautious failure. When you make yourself vulnerable and put yourself in a place of utter dependency upon God you will see His power manifested in response to your faith, and that is simply awesome. We need to see God's hand in our life. We need to see Him demonstrate His power. There are some who say "We walk by faith, we do not need to see a manifestation of His power." That is the talk of a cautious failure. Anyone who has seen the power of God would never make such a silly statement. In all my years as a believer I've never yet seen anyone who wasn't excited, ecstatic even, when God's power has been revealed in response to their faith. God wants us to experience His power. Seeing and experiencing God's power emboldens us to do greater things in His service.

Spontaneity: the key to the release of God's power.

In the book of Psalms it is written, *"Thy people will volunteer freely in the day of Thy power; In holy array, from the womb of the dawn, Thy youth are to Thee as the dew" (Psalm 110:3).* When God manifests His power the people He uses will be a special kind of people; as this verse puts it they will be a people who 'volunteer freely.' In another version of the bible the phrase is translated 'be willing,' and when you look up its meaning in the original Hebrew you find it is 'spontaneity.' Peter's act in walking on water was spontaneous, and spontaneity is the key to the release of God's power.

Spontaneous people are the ones who will participate and experience the power of God, described here in the psalm as 'God's youth.' Nike's advertising philosophy 'just do it' captures the essence of spontaneity. It is no wonder it is directed toward the young, after all spontaneity is typical of the youth who are responsive and eager. They need little prompting or persuading because they are not tied down, nor are they settled in their ways or rooted in some tradition. These are the qualities God is looking for when He does a new thing.

Was Peter impetuous or spontaneous? Through the years conventional wisdom suggest he was impetuous. I say it was spontaneity that defined Peter's character. And spontaneity is the key to the release of God's power.

Just do it.

Looking Up To Heaven

chapter eight

> *And ordering the multitudes to recline on the grass, He took the five loaves and the two fish, and looking up toward heaven, He blessed the food, and breaking the loaves he gave them to the disciples, and the disciples gave to the multitudes, and they all ate and were satisfied.*
> **(Mathew 14:19,20)**

Jesus took the food, blessed it, then broke it and distributed the portions. Five loaves and two fish, insufficient for a few people, much less a multitude. How many of us would have considered sharing those meager resources with the crowd? Yet Jesus unhesitatingly distributed the food and fed a multitude. In the act of giving, the few loaves and fishes were multiplied and were more than adequate to feed a large crowd. An ordinary meal was turned into an extraordinary event. Scripture doesn't tell us the how of the miracle, only the fact.

If a spiritual principle can be drawn from this episode in Jesus' ministry it is this; give the little you have now. Not later, but now. Instead of waiting until you have an abundance, share the little you already have at hand. Take your guitar to the worship meeting, even if you can only play a few chords. Call in and visit that one who is lonely, take a few minutes you can ill afford out of your busy week. A Christian is a giver and ought not to refrain from sharing because they don't have much to offer. If we let opportunities for giving slip by we will never become givers. There are people in the church with talent and ability, but you would never know it because they haven't practiced giving. Oh, sure, if pressed into service they are obliging. But they never volunteer, they have to be drawn out. There must always be a request before they give. So their character is marked by a withholding of self.

On the other hand there are people in the church without any notable talent who are always there in the forefront when there is a need. On their shoulders God builds His church. They carry the burden of work. You may not be much in your own estimation but if you tell yourself you're waiting until such time as you have more to offer, you deprive God of the opportunity to feed the hungry now. Give the little you have and trust God to make up any deficiency.

It would be premature to conclude the moral of this story is only about always being willing to lend a helping hand. This isn't just a lesson to encourage us toward generosity. This is a story about a miracle. First and foremost it is a demonstration of the creative power of God multiplying something far beyond the original form in which it was given. The disciples had taken stock of their resources - five loaves and two fish - and concluded naturally enough there was not enough to feed the large crowd. They proposed Jesus dismiss the crowd so they might go and find something to eat. Master teacher that He was Jesus used the occasion as an opportunity to demonstrate to the disciples they had reckoned without the resources of heaven. "They do not need to go away; you give them something to eat," Jesus said.

When the disciples failed to act Jesus did. As Jesus blessed the food and prepared to distribute the portions, the Bible record of the event uses the interesting phrase "and looking up toward heaven." I would suggest these words are of deep significance and go far beyond simply indicating the direction of Jesus gaze as He blessed the food. His upward glance was not incidental, but rather the outward manifestation of the inner reality of His life; Jesus lived in the awareness of the ever present availability of God's power. He looked upward to God as was His habit. Jesus looked upward to heaven from whence came the manna to feed the children of Israel in the wilderness. He looked upward with complete assurance Yahweh would intervene in this situation in like manner. His looking upward was entirely natural. Just as my young children turn to me to meet their wants, it carries the same expectation born out of past experiences in bringing needs to a father and seeing them comprehensively met.

Where is our gaze habitually directed? Heavenward or earthward? The question is significant because the direction of our gaze suggests what is meaningful and important in our lives. The object of our contemplation shapes our thinking and defines our worldview. If our gaze is earthward our expectations will be earthy - and minimal. We are unlikely to see water gush from a rock, or manna fall from the skies when our boundaries are limited by the visible and felt commonplace things that make up our everyday experiences. So long as our gaze is horizontal we will likely only ever see the ordinary and mundane. How often in everyday life do we look up? Really look up? We say grace before a meal with our heads bowed. In the act of acknowledging God's provision our body language suggests we see earth as the source. We talk of the separation of church and state and tacitly accept a view of life that separates and distinguishes the spiritual from the practical. This mentality carries over into our everyday life, as we give God Sunday while keeping the rest of the week for ourselves. So long as our gaze is earthward - even though we invoke the name of God - our expectations will be commonplace. It is unlikely we will ever see the power of God displayed in a wondrous manifestation of supernatural power.

Taking the few loaves and fishes Jesus looked up to heaven. As I read these words I am simultaneously challenged and inspired. Jesus took what was at hand! That's all any of us need to bring - only what we have at hand - nothing more. The disciples were ordinary working men, like you and me. They were not chosen because they possessed some advantage over their contemporaries; they were not wealthy men, they had no special status in their community. They had no religious training, they were not of proven character, nor did they possess any exceptional talent which made them more suitable candidates for discipleship. Nothing about these twelve men made them stand out from their peers or set them apart in terms of religious zeal. The only thing that set them apart was they were called to follow Jesus. In this timeless story Jesus is saying to every Believer; "I've called you and placed you where you are. You can handle whatever comes your way. All I ask of you is to give what you have and look up." God only wants us to give what we can. As we do this we make the wonderful discovery that as we do so and look up, our meager offering in God's hands is more than enough. In the words of the biblical scholar William Barclay, "Come to me as you are, however ill equipped, bring what you have, however little, I will use it greatly in My service." In preaching the gospel we are going to find ourselves out of our depth. We will be called upon to meet the needs of desperate people who have nowhere left to turn for help. We will be expected to provide counsel in situations for which there are no easy answers. We will bring hope into places where there is no hope. Where darkness and death abound we will bring light and life. This is the tremendous task we undertake as we accept the great commission to go forth into the world, and it does not demand from us an eminence we do not possess.

While at Ben Israel Ministries I and some other students were fortunate enough to accompany Art on a ministry trip throughout Europe as he preached in various churches. In Italy some Christians in communist Yugoslavia he knew from previous visits contacted him requesting he alter his plans and visit them. An urgent need had arisen relating to a young man. This Yugoslav Christian had been seen as one of the bright stars of the fledgling church in that communist country, but unhappily he had committed adultery with another church member's wife and had fallen away from the church. Now the young man discovered he had cancer. His friends in the church were requesting we meet with the man.

So we were headed off in our vehicle from Ugano to Trieste to make the visit. As we traveled I wondered what on earth the minister would say to this young man who had a sentence of death over him and apparently believed it to be a punishment from God. What were his expectations of us in seeking this meeting? Was he hoping we would pray for him to be healed? Was he expecting Art to pronounce forgiveness? Apparently he viewed Art as a spiritual father and esteemed him as a man close to God.

Obviously then, so far as this person was concerned, anything Art said would be taken as a pronouncement from God. But Art himself confided on the way that he had not heard from God and had formed no opinion on the matter. As we crossed the country in our van he vouchsafed he had not the slightest inkling of what to say.

I prayed about it as we traveled but got no sense whatsoever of God's view in the matter. I pondered the dilemma as we moved across the border into Yugoslavia and nearer our destination. What if this cancer was a judgement of God upon the man for his sins? If so, there would be no use praying for his healing. On the other hand, because of the way this man looked up to Art, his opinion would carry a weight. If he so much as opinioned the cancer might be God's judgement it would be tantamount to destroying what little hope the man might have and prove a crushing blow at a time when he desperately needed encouragement. It seemed to me an awful burden to put on anyone that the words in their mouth should be considered as a pronouncement from the Lord. I had a mental image of sitting down with this man and his friends and as they looked confidently and expectantly to Art, the man of God simply sitting there looking blankly back at them with no word from the Lord. Maybe it would have been wiser not to have come rather than create some expectancy by coming only to be a disappointment. Like the disciples I had taken stock of my resources and was ready to send them away to fend for themselves. If as Christians we've habitually faced every challenge out of our own resources, then we either avoid people in dire straits or send them away to find help elsewhere. Like most people I am ready enough to help if my contribution can make a difference. It is the overwhelming need that is daunting.

My worst fears were realized when we met the little group waiting for us on a street in the inner city where we had arranged to meet. Three very apprehensive people stood huddled together clutching each other as if for support. The man with two of his friends, all who had been led to the Lord by Art, gathered around him like children meeting their father after a long absence. Crying and laughing they hugged and clustered about him all the time touching him, unwilling to let him go. It was clear by the emotional welcome that Art's coming represented an answer to prayer. It was clear by the look in their faces he was their hope. He would tell them what to do. He would make all things clear. They were looking to him for answers. And I knew what they didn't - that he had no answers.

I don't remember anything outstanding about that day. Nothing profound was spoken. No great pearl of wisdom, no thunderclaps of revelation from God. We walked and talked. We looked in shop windows and I marveled at the scarcity of goods in this communist state, what little was on display, antiquated, twenty years out of date. We sat in their apartment and talked. They were very serious, hanging on every word. Questions, answers from scripture. We prayed. We ate - a baked apple! They didn't eat I noticed, I suspect because there were no more apples. And when we left, no false assurances had been given. Just the word of God in response to each concern and fear they shared. And it was enough, it reassured them. When we left they were at peace, all the anxiety was gone. We gave little, but in God's hands it was more than enough. We left them laughing and crying just as when we arrived. But it was a different sort of tears. Tears of joy. Tears of release from pent up anxieties.

Throughout the miracle of the loaves and fishes Jesus actions are calculated and deliberate. He sets the stage, then

He acts. His actions would be presumptuous unless He were confident God's help would be forthcoming. He gathered the food available and had the crowd recline on the ground. Only He and a few disciples knew that what he was holding in His hand wasn't enough to go around. The question we must ask ourselves in the face of each need that comes our way is, "What stops us from giving now?" Very often it is because the need is overwhelming and we are ill equipped to help. What do you say to someone who just lost three children in a car accident? What do you say to someone whose marriage you know is falling apart? How do you work toward reconciliation between Bosnians and the Serbs while just down the road the international peace keeping forces are digging up mass graves of victims tortured and murdered in that bloody civil war? The last thing we want to do in such situations is raise a false hope.

Jesus does not want us to be daunted by overwhelming needs. If we measure what we have to offer against the need it may seem pathetically inadequate. But the decision to give must not be made by weighing the effectiveness of our contribution. As you and I practice giving the little we have and looking up to God, the One who ultimately meets every need, we begin to see that in God's hands our small offering makes a difference. To give from a sense of inadequacy is to appreciate that whether I give much or little is unimportant, because I don't meet the need, God does. We ought always to keep this truth uppermost: God does not expect us to satisfy the need. He will meet the need. A failure to appreciate this subtle distinction is very often the reason we withhold our help. As Christian's we have at our disposal the infinite resources of a heavenly Father. When Jesus exhorted His disciple with the words, "They do not need to go away; you give them something to eat," He wanted them to know the few morsel's they had to offer could become a feast as God multiplied them.

It Takes Guts To Say "Jesus."

chapter nine

A story concerning a Christian student and an atheist professor of philosophy that had made its rounds over the internet, ended up in my email. It seems the professor, in a class he took on logic, spent the semester trying to prove that God did not exist. At the end he would challenge his students by asking if anyone still believed that God existed. Over the years no one in his class had ever admitted to being a Christian. Our student would have avoided the class if he could, but it was a required course and he had no choice. He prayed much that he would have the courage to stand up for his faith when the time came. When the semester came to an end, the professor asked if there was any student who still believed in God. Our student raised his hand. The professor called him a fool and said if God existed he could stop this piece of chalk he held in his hand from smashing when he dropped it. As he let it go, the chalk slipped out of his fingers, into his shirt cuff, down the pleat of his trousers where it rolled onto his shoe, and thence to the floor where it rolled away unbroken. According to the story, which I have no idea whether it is fact or fiction, the professor made a quick exit and the student stayed behind to share the gospel to the class.

The theme of our tale is about publicly confessing our faith, not always an easy thing to do. Of the need for public confession of our faith in Him, Jesus Himself had this to say, *"Everyone therefore who shall confess Me before men, I will also confess him before My Father who is in heaven"* (Matthew 10:32). We cannot remain quiet about our faith. Those who declare that religion is a private matter do not have scripture to back up their assertion. Our public confession of Jesus is the condition upon which Jesus owns us before the Father. In his classic formulae for salvation the apostle Paul linked confession with belief - *"if you confess with your mouth Jesus as Lord, and believe in your heart that God raised Him from the dead, you shall be saved"* (Romans 10:9).

Our student was an unlikely hero for he had no desire for the confrontation. An apologist might relish the thought of publicly debating an atheist professor before an audience. For a young student not used to the spotlight and unsure of his theology it would be a daunting prospect. The setting was hugely weighted in the favor of the professor, operating in a familiar environment with an audience primed and receptive to his point of view. Our student was afraid of the certain public humiliation. Had it been at all possible he would have skipped taking this class altogether. But he couldn't; if he wanted to major in his chosen subject, he had to take this class and face the challenge to confess his faith before the atheist professor.

This test of faith is inevitable for every person who names the name of Jesus as Lord. There is a day, an appointed hour, a moment when you and I too will be dared to stand up for Jesus and confess Him publicly. The inevitability of this future provocation lies in the Bible's observation that the world is fundamentally hostile to Jesus. Therefore we can expect in the ordinary course of our lives sooner or later to find ourselves facing the dilemma the student found himself in. Either we must stand up and declare our allegiance to Christ before a skeptical, possibly hostile audience, or remain silent in our seat. If we're painfully honest, how many of us can identify times in the past when the opportunity was there to declare our allegiance to Jesus, but we kept our mouth shut. The thought of the raised eyebrow, the sideways glance, what people might think about us, was too intimidating and we kept to ourselves the message that people need to hear.

None of us know when the challenge will next be placed before us to publicly confess our faith. Then again perhaps we can make a fairly good guess. Possibly it will mean no longer turning a blind eye to the boss at work who cheats the customers, or the employee who cheats their employer. At school it may require taking an unpopular Biblical view in regard to some ethical issue. Conceivably it could be a lunch table confrontation with the blasphemer at work. The student in our story came out as a hero. It is just as likely our public confession will bring jeers and vilification. The consequence for our fidelity to Christ may well cost us credibility and friendships, perhaps our job, possibly ostracism from our own family. If we balk at this we should note the price in the past has been much higher - the blood of martyrs who died for confessing.

Many Believers have never made a public profession of faith. Hoping to slip through life unnoticed, they remain quiet and unobtrusive when the opportunity is presented in the public domain to say the name of Jesus. One commentator said unequivocally this is tantamount to denying Him; "Public confession of Christ is an indispensable requirement of salvation. The want of courage to confess is decisive evidence of the heart to believe."*

An unlikely hero

If we feel like hanging our head in shame, there is cause for hope. I want to take a look at another unlikely hero. God's man of the hour at the most crucial and pivotal event in the history of mankind was a secret disciple who, like the student in our story, had to overcome his fear before publicly confessing Jesus.

The tumultuous events of the first Easter weekend are well known; the band of Jews and Roman soldiers led by Judas came in the night holding forth their flickering lanterns, weapons at the ready. The disciples wakened out of their sleep put up a token resistance before fleeing into the early morning darkness. Once Jesus was taken into custody events moved swiftly to trial and crucifixion. None of the disciples were able to recover and organize themselves in response to the disaster. Peter, disorientated by the dramatic turn events had taken and unable to gather himself, denied his master three times in the course of that evening. But one disciple did gather himself, and his resolute and bold action that weekend was in marked contrast to the other disciples' vacillating and cowardice. One disciple stood by Jesus on that first Easter weekend. One man was up to the occasion. A very unlikely hero, he didn't fit the stereotype of Jesus' disciples. In the first place he was a wealthy man, he wasn't from the poor working class who made up most of Jesus followers. He hadn't left his home and family to follow Jesus as the inner group of disciples had. This man hadn't given up anything for Jesus.

*(Commentary on the Epistle To The Romans, Charles Hodge. P 343, 344).

It Takes Guts to Say "Jesus"

Wealthy man that he was, it is quite possible he never supported Jesus ministry with financial contributions, but if he did, one thing is certain, few if any knew about it. Indeed it is very unlikely anyone acquainted with Jesus, including His closest disciples, would even have recognized this man as a follower.

He took care to remain out of the limelight, away from the immediate entourage who constantly surrounded Jesus. He was never a part of that noisy, bustling throng who pressed Jesus with questions. He was always on the fringe of the crowds who came to listen to Jesus, rather than near the front. Our mystery man took good care not to be associated with Jesus. It is quite possible he never spoke a word to Jesus, but he heard Jesus speak. Oh, yes, he heard Jesus speak and when he did his heart was aglow with the words he heard. Aside from his wealth one other distinguishing feature set this disciple apart from the other disciples and made him unique. This man was a leader in the nation of Israel, well known and respected by the majority of people. He had political power. In point of fact he was a distinguished member of the Sanhedrin. Yes, he was a part of the ruling body of Jews who tried and condemned Jesus to death. The group described in John's gospel as 'the Jews,' the political and religious establishment in Israel who were Jesus' sworn enemies.

This is the reason why our mystery man kept his admiration for Jesus secret. He was afraid of his peers finding out. He feared the repercussions that would come if it came out he was a follower of Jesus. So he kept it very quiet. The Bible says he kept his discipleship secret for fear of the Jews. In modern idiom we would say he was a closet disciple. If you haven't guessed by now, I am referring to Joseph of Arimathea. Joseph was the man who went in and asked Pilate for Jesus' body and gave it a proper burial in his own tomb. In doing so he came out in the open and declared his allegiance to Jesus. Joseph was not the stuff of which hero's are made. He was an altogether unlikely hero.

All four gospel accounts of the crucifixion describe Joseph's role. It is the only time the Bible mentions him. He is not heard of before or after. He makes his appearance on the most momentous occasion in history and is gone. But without him the resurrection story would not come down to us in the form we know so well. One commentator says criminal's bodies were not usually given proper burial but were simply thrown into a pit. Another commentator said it would have taken someone of Joseph's prestige and power to get an audience with Pilate and be permitted to take the body. Joseph provided the tomb for Jesus' body which his followers found empty save for the folded grave clothes on that first Easter Sunday. By placing Jesus body safely away from interference and covering it with a huge stone he inadvertently provided irrefutable proof of Jesus resurrection. The details of the Easter message come down to us as a result of Joseph. By his action in going before Pilate, Joseph came out of the closet and made clear his support for Jesus. There is heavy irony in these events. At a time when Peter was beside himself with remorse for having cowardly denied being a follower of Jesus, another who previously kept quiet his discipleship was busy owning Him. Peter and his fellow disciples who had bravely suffered the reproach and animosity of the ruling Jews to loyally support Jesus' ministry (and who had just days earlier professed they would lay down their lives for Jesus), lost heart in Jesus hour of need and abandoned Him. It was left to Joseph, who didn't stand by Jesus while He was alive, to do so when He died. The crisis produced startling and unpredictable effects; fear from those you would expect courage, and courage from one in whom you would expect fear. Quite a turn around for the books, isn't it?

A well known football coach wrote, "As a football coach I've seen two common barriers that most often prevent people from performing to their fullest potential; a pattern of past failure and mistakes, and, a fear of failure." People who drop the ball are not called off the bench to make critical plays when time is running out on the clock. Coaches look for someone who is reliable with a solid record when a big play has to be made. Joseph's background of failure does not commend himself as a natural choice a coach would make in a similar situation. Imagine if you can all Jesus followers sitting on a football bench in the Garden of Gethsemane. A little distance away but within earshot, Jesus is praying for the strength to go through the fate that is about to befall Him. It is a tense situation. No one is really sure what the morrow will bring, but it is clear from the Master's agonizing prayer courage of exceptional caliber will be required. Imagine further you are the coach, you know each and every disciple intimately, even the secret ones like Joseph, and out of all Jesus followers you have to pick out one person who can be counted on to stand by Jesus. As you cast your eyes down the bench of disciples you wouldn't even give Joseph a second glance. As you weighed your decision your eyes would probably rove to and fro over the twelve disciples. "These" you would say to yourself, "have stood by Jesus from the beginning and have remained true to Him throughout the hostility of the authorities. They have already demonstrated a willingness to suffer for Him." Finally your eyes would settle on one of the twelve. "He is the one," you would say to yourself. "He is the one who is a natural leader, he is the one who is first to grasp things and more than any other disciple demonstrated bold faith."

Out loud you would say, "Peter, you are the one. Get out there on the field."

But God chose Joseph and we know what happened to Peter, don't we? He dropped the ball in the biggest play in history. You could say God completely abandoned conventional wisdom in His choice of a player to carry the ball. When the scripted play called for confrontation God chose someone who had previously been intimidated. When it might cost everything to stand by Jesus, God chose a man who had shown no inclination to do so in the past. You could say God used a failure at the most pivotal point in history. And you would be right. The man of the hour who took control and center stage was a failure as a disciple.

Yet the wisdom of God's choice was vindicated. How can we explain this? The key to understanding this unexpected display of courage lies in the fact that you cannot take faith for granted.

Have you heard someone express the thought, "I wish I had your faith?" 'To have faith' is a misleading expression. It makes faith seem like a personal quality that makes some of us uniquely suited to the role of bearing an effective Christian witness, in much the same way that a superior football player has sure hand-eye coordination. Such a view of faith imagines we all have faith to varying degrees, some more so than others. The truth is, while each and every Believer is expected to live by faith, the source of faith lies outside of ourselves in God. He supplies faith, and He sustains faith. No one has an inherent advantage when it comes to faith. Faith must always be sought anew if we are to meet the challenge of living for Christ. It is never something we can assume. The disciples closest to Jesus were complacent in those crucial days and hours leading up to Jesus arrest; "We will not forsake you," they protested. "Never," they repeated emphatically. "I will never

It Takes Guts to Say "Jesus"

deny you," Peter argued vehemently with Jesus. And of course in the garden when Jesus asked them to watch and pray with Him that they would not fall into temptation, they fell asleep. The disciples were confident in their faith, confident in their ability to handle any situation that called upon them to defend their master. Because they were complacent they failed utterly in the crisis.

Sooner or later every Christian makes the discovery that this walk of faith God has called them to is far beyond what they imagined. They discover the personal qualities which they imagined faith rested upon - virtues such as courage, loyalty, affection - go nowhere near far enough in allowing them to live up to God's holy calling. The old testament prophet Isaiah despaired of his unworthiness crying out, "Woe is me. I am a man of unclean lips." Paul the apostle cried out in despair, "Who is sufficient for these things." The psalmist wrote eloquently of his love for God's law and at the same time was disheartened by his inability to live up to it.

It is good to know in spiritual matters you are weak. People such as Joseph who have not lived up to or become worthy of their calling have already confronted this painful reality. They know they are weak, easily intimidated, very conscious that they do not perform well under stress. Past experience tells them that there is a very good likelihood they will let God down. A sense of personal inadequacy, far from being a negative, is a rich deposit going into the life of faith. The person who has failed has one important advantage, they are very conscious of their limitations. They are not likely to labor under any illusions about themselves. If the failure has wrought them an awareness of their weakness that drives them to their knees in prayer to call upon a power greater than they possess, then they are in good shape, the right shape for maintaining faith - an utter awareness of their dependence on God. Of all the disciples that weekend, Joseph more than any other knew his faith was not up to it. Of all the disciples his was the only faith that was up to it.

If God is for us, who is against us? (Romans 8:31).

To the person of trembling faith, overwhelmed by the magnitude of the task they are called upon to perform, God promises His support: "Even to your old age, I shall be the same, And even to your graying years I shall bear you! I have done it, and I shall carry you; And I shall bear you, and I shall deliver you" (Isaiah 46:4). Paul made the same assertion to the Roman church when he declared his confidence in a group within the church who were considered weak in the faith and unlikely to amount to anything. To those in the church who were tempted to write these saints off, Paul reminded them they had not taken into consideration the fact that God under-girded them. "And stand he will, for the Lord is able to make him stand" (Romans 14:4) . God has a stake in whether a person overcomes and the confident affirmation of Paul for the weak Christian is made on the basis of the Lord's interest in the outcome. It is God's enabling power, not the strength of the Christian, upon which this promise is founded.

The Bible does not tell us much detail about Joseph. We only know he was a failure as a disciple for want of courage. The Bible tells us even at the end he was afraid because he had to pluck up courage and ask Pilate for Jesus' body. But I rather think of him like the student in the story; knowing his weakness he prayed and asked God that he might not fail Jesus. In the dark hours of that first Easter weekend when all seemed lost to Jesus' disciples, Joseph's faith grew strong. Something happened that caused Joseph to come out in the open and declare his allegiance to Jesus. Joseph was present in the Sanhedrin court hastily assembled in the early morning hours to try Jesus. We know this for the Bible record tells us he did not vote to crucify Jesus. I like to think that perhaps that was the first time Joseph saw Jesus close up. In the past it was always from a distance, on the fringe of the crowd pressing around Jesus. Perhaps much of Jesus' works were relayed to him second hand by a confidant, and what he heard thrilled his heart with the thought that this was indeed the long promised Messiah. Now as Jesus was being tried he saw Him close up and watching Jesus demeanor, seeing the dignity with which he conducted Himself before the court, he saw in Jesus something so lovely, so true, his heart was won over completely. Perhaps he caught Jesus' eye and there passed between them an unspoken communication. It is not unlikely Joseph would have felt a secret shame for having failed to support Jesus. His mind maybe was a swirl of thoughts, wishing he could go back in time and have the opportunity to make amends somehow, and in the midst of these jumbling, rushing, tumbling thoughts Jesus glanced at him and Joseph read unqualified acceptance and unconditional love. In that moment he determined to do for Christ in death what he never could do for Him in life.

Now that might be an entirely fanciful account of events. However, it is not exaggerated or far fetched to say that Jesus' last encounter with Joseph sparked the boldness his faith had always lacked to confess Jesus. In the end, Jesus who inspired Joseph's faith, was responsible for consummating it. What the incarnate Jesus was to Joseph, the glorified Christ will be to you and me today. Hebrews 12:2 describes Him as 'the author and perfecter of faith'. As High Priest he sits at the right hand of the Father interceding for the saints. The same Jesus who inspired my faith and your faith has undertaken to care for our faith. What that means in practical terms is this: when a situation arises that staggers our faith, as it surely will, Christ, who waits for our faith to come through and perform, is a Savior who Himself will care for our faith at that moment. Reflect upon that thought for a moment and let the wonder of it sink in. Jesus, who finished the work of faith he began in Joseph, will do the same for us. He will bring to maturity and completion the overcoming faith you and I need to bear an effective and bold witness for Him.

The Righteous Live by Their Faith.

chapter ten

Going home.

Our year at Ben Israel Ministries in northern Minnesota was almost up and from beginning to end we had had a wonderful time. Coming from a temperate climate it was a novelty waking in the morning to the sound of the oil fired furnace and looking out the window at a blanket of white. Crunching through the snow we made our way after breakfast to the trailer we used for classes. It was so cold in the sub zero temperatures that our eyelids stuck together when we blinked.

Each Friday night the whole community came together for shabot, which the Jewish believers within the community celebrated. The diversity of nationalities represented by the students and the frequent visitors made for a lively and entertaining time of fellowship. At some part in the evening someone would start strumming a guitar and there would be an impromptu time of worship, one song flowing into the other interspersed with spontaneous prayers of praise and thanksgiving.

We were welcomed from the start and made to feel at home. Jan and I even had our own trailer comfortably furnished, right next door to Art and Inger Katz' house. Often when I looked next door I was reminded of Art's words to us when we first approached him about coming to Ben Israel, "We do not have any facilities for you to stay." Jan and I had been prepared to sleep apart, in dormitories if necessary, instead we had our very own private quarters ten yards from Art's back door. Maybe God has a sense of humor. Our reputation preceded our arrival because of the letter I had written challenging Ben Israel to begin the school in spite of a lack of facilities. Said one person to us, "I will never forget the day Art Beebe (one of three elders at Ben Israel Ministries) came running out of his trailer holding your letter up and waving it in his hand." Yes, it was our letter that got the school off the ground and that was a wonderful fillip to our faith.

On arrival I went to Art Beebe and told him how little money we had, not enough to support ourselves for a year. He put me at ease straight away with the kindly and reassuring remark that everyone in the community pitched in together and all looked to the Lord for their provision. So we pitched in. In the morning we had classes, and in the afternoons worked for the ministry or on the farm property. Like everyone in the community we got free board and food in lieu of wages.

After anticipating this trip for so long it might easily have been a let down. It exceeded all our expectations, an adventure from beginning to end, really a mountain top experience. With no money of our own and as tourists unable to earn any income we saw God provide for us beyond what we ever expected. The highlight was a ministry trip overseas to Europe, the Middle East, and Africa. We went to Israel, visited Jerusalem, stood on the Mount of

The Righteous Live by Their Faith

Olives where Jesus stood, marveled at how small it was for a mountain; why, it was no more than a hill. From the Mount of Olives we walked the route Jesus probably took on His ride into Jerusalem just across the valley. Olive trees at the bottom of the Mount of Olives, we were told, were 2000 years old, they could well have been there in Jesus time. As I stood in one grove of trees I mused that maybe this was the very garden of Gethsemane where Jesus prayed the night he was arrested. The tree I was touching could well have been a silent witness to Jesus' agonized prayer on the eve of His crucifixion when He asked His Father to remove, if possible, His cup of suffering.

That year at Ben Israel Ministries was a very special year. It was hard not to escape the feeling we were special, selected and set apart by God for a special purpose, right on the cutting edge of what God was doing. Yes, it was a mountain top year, but as they say you can go from the mountain to the valley in a moment. For Jan and me our stay in the USA ended like Jack and Jill: we came tumbling down off the mountain.

Our visa was up and it was time to go home. But of course we had no return ticket. Without money or a credit card with which to buy one we had a problem. During our heady year, seeing so many provisions of God it was hard to imagine He hadn't foreseen this contingency. We saw the miracle of our coming into the States, we would see the miracle of God's provision again going home. Who knows, maybe we weren't going back to New Zealand just yet. We sensed God had more for us in the USA. Said one person in the community to us, "You and Jan are different from the other students, you seem to belong here." Could that be why God only provided a one way ticket? Did He perhaps intend to open the door for some ministry opportunity in the USA, if not at Ben Israel then perhaps another of the fellowships we visited? Nothing materialized, however, and so the time came to go home. The plan was that we would accompany Art and Mary Beebe on a ministry trip they were making to the west coast. They would take us to Vancouver, Canada, where I would visit an aunt whom I had never met before flying home. I said nothing to them about not having a ticket or money, determined to trust God. All the way across the States I prayed for God to provide the money to be able to buy a ticket for our trip home. In hindsight Jan and I have discussed whether our silence was a mistake. I know the people at Ben Israel would have given us their last penny. However I was also keenly aware they were themselves often in financial straits and did not wish to burden them with our problems. When things do not work out you tend to second guess every decision and act to find out if there is a reason why faith didn't work. In the months to come I would do a lot of such thinking.

We made our way west stopping at various fellowships along the way. The last stop on our journey was a small fellowship in Washington state where we visited for a few days. Then the morning came to leave for Vancouver and the rendezvous with my Aunt, where Art and Mary would take their leave of us and continue on their way.

You take faith as far as you can. Trusting God all the way. Until you come to a dead end and can go no further. Either a way will open up or it will not, God will provide or He will not. But you do not stop before that. You do not want the reproach of hearing God say you stopped short.

Disaster! The Canadian border official asked if everyone in the car were American. When told that two of us were New Zealanders he wanted to know the purpose of our trip. When Art replied we were planning to stay and visit an aunt in Vancouver before flying back to New Zealand the official asked to see our ticket out of the country. Well of course we couldn't produce one. Unable to do so he refused to let us in without proof we would make good on our intention. I will never forget that drive back down interstate five toward Seattle. I was devastated. I had messed up Art and Mary's plans, along with an aunt who was waiting to meet me back in Vancouver. At some point Jan began to cry. I have a memory of travelling along interstate five seeing the tops of fully grown trees beside the road on an overpass. They looked strange, the tops of trees poking above the side of the road, I had never seen that before. Odd the things that stick in your mind in a calamity - no memory of anything Art or Mary said on that long trip, just the trees and Jan crying. I have never felt such a helpless feeling as I felt at that moment stranded in a foreign country. I have put people to trouble and upset their plans. I do not know what is going to happen, where I will stay that night, what we will do or how we will get home. Jan's quiet sobs drive home to me the helplessness of our predicament.

When things do not go right we remind ourselves God's ways are higher than ours. If there is any comfort in those words it is in the thought that things are not as they seem. God is in control and His plan for our life continues. I did not know it then but the events taking place that day were a key in God's plan to bring us back to the USA to live. I would come to see this disaster in a whole new light, and marvel at God's ways, but that would be some years away.

Disappointed and confounded.

It is becoming common to see some sports players on TV take the opportunity after a triumph to acknowledge their faith in Jesus Christ. After scoring the touchdown in the NFL the player goes down on one knee, the camera catches him frozen, finger pointing heavenward, his head bowed. 'Thank you Jesus.' After winning the NBA title in 1998 San Antonio players shouted into the cameras, "Jesus takes care of those who are His." Another time, another player, another championship game, the Final Fours on the way to the college basketball championship. As the camera zeroed in on him he spoke excitedly about how faith in God had kept this team through the season. He talked about having a dream, of believing in his dream, of overcoming adversity and concluded triumphantly, "the righteous live by faith."

The moral is we are winners if we have Jesus. We all want that winner's testimony, don't we? "I just want to thank the Lord because without Him this victory would not have been possible." The classic testimony we always hear can be broken down into a few basic components: I had a dream, I stuck to it through adversity, through all the trials and tribulations I kept the faith and God kept me. Finally triumph, and faith is vindicated. The speaker concludes, "To God be the glory, praise the Lord," and he punches his fist in the air while the audience applauds.

Now I admire those sportsmen who take the occasion of their triumph to honor God. If it is done on prime TV for millions to see, so much the better. When things are good and you are winning it is easy to declare your faith in God. But I can't help wondering what happens to the Christian on the losing team. Let us imagine there was such a player who since he was a little boy had dreamed of winning the final four. Throughout his college years he honored God. His faith kept the dream alive when times were tough, but instead of celebrating a victory he is lying on the court where moments earlier he watched his shot that would have won the game spin around the rim and fall outside the basket. If faith is all about winning in life, then losers not only go home without a trophy to put on their shelf, they just lost their testimony. This young basketball player must come to terms with a God who denied him his happiness.

Losers who have put their trust in God are left to wrestle with deep theological questions. "Why, God?" were the poignant words on one of many flower arrangements at the funeral for a murdered child. The implication is that God failed the little girl, He was not there for her when she needed protection. A pastor's wife writes tragically in a magazine of how her husband ran off with another woman after they had labored together for years in God's work. Why God? In the genre of literature arising out of the holocaust, when six million Jews perished in the ovens of Hitler's Germany, "Why God?" is a very strong motif.

Maybe the failure of God to provide a ticket home is merely a speed bump on the road of life compared to the murder of a child. The trauma of losing a basketball game can scarcely be compared with seeing your entire family wiped out in the holocaust. Nevertheless at root they are dealing with the same issue, a crisis of faith. God was not there for us when we expected Him to be. All of His promises of providential care were not able to prevent the disappointment which came into our lives. Being in a relationship with Him did not make us special. He was not a Savior to us when we needed saving. Was he unable to bring to a successful conclusion the dreams we entrusted into his care? I remember praying, "Lord it was within your power to help, why did you not intervene? If we were presumptuous in our faith, could you in your mercy not have shown us the error?" After all we were in America in the first place because He had led us there, surely we are justified in expecting his provision when we were being obedient to His will. Doesn't He promise to provide our every need? Doesn't His word tell us to trust Him? Doesn't Jesus say if you ask in faith, believing, you shall receive? We had faith! We believed! Besides we had seen God miraculously get us into the United States. His failure to act to provide a way home was confounding. Based upon our understanding of Him and the promises in His word, He should have acted on our behalf. The apparent contradiction between God's revealed word to us and our tragedy exacerbates the painful experience. Disappointed and confused, we pose the question, "Why God? Why did you not intervene? You could have done something. It doesn't make sense."

Except for a select few players, the road to the championship ends in disappointment. Is this what it all comes down to for those who put their hopes in God? A few will win, the greater majority of us will have to come to terms with shattered hoop dreams? Are there limits to faith? Or to put it another way, does God care about our hopes? Our basketball hero in his moment of victory declared that the righteous live by faith. But maybe God had nothing to do with the victory. Maybe one team was better than the other, maybe it was just fate, the bounce of the ball determined the winner. A good many persons are sympathetic to a faith that helps a person through life, but hostile toward a radical faith that expects God to intervene directly to affect the outcome. A doctor might agree faith can help a patient recover from an illness, but would deny God could or would supernaturally heal a person. Is that all faith is - just another word for positive thinking?

My faith was radical. Was it discredited? An unbeliever would say, "absolutely." How do you go on in the faith when God's word has not held up in your life? The unbeliever

The Righteous Live by Their Faith

would say these circumstances are proof (if ever proof was needed) that you can not rely on God. In the mind of the unbelieving Jewish writer the holocaust is all the proof he needs that faith in a God who intervenes in the affairs of men is unfounded. For if ever there was a time God needed to act for His name's sake this was it. When His people, those who are called by His name, to whom He gave His covenants and promises, were hauled off and burnt in the ovens, six million of them, and the God of Abraham did nothing to prevent it. So the unbelieving Jewish writer justifies his action of refraining from worship declaring in offended dignity, "I can't believe a loving God would ever allow that to happen."

What is the word of God when we reach the end of the road? The Bible is unequivocal; in these situations the solution is *more faith*. Scripture is very clear: faith is not an option. Whatever life deals us, we are to live by faith. Whether it is the loser in a basketball tournament or a woman grieving a pastor husband who ran off and left her, or whether it is a young couple stranded without a plane ticket, or a Jew who lost all his family in a holocaust, God's word is the same, *"but the righteous man shall live by faith" (Romans 1:17)*. To the unbeliever it stretches credibility to the absurd. "You fool, you poor blind fool. God's promises did nothing to save you in the past. Are you going to make yourself vulnerable again and open yourself up to further disappointment?" Those who are unable to reconcile the contradiction between the events in their life with their understanding of God's Word, are very vulnerable to the powerful persuasive logic of unbelievers which says no one, not even God, has power to guarantee our well being, much less bring about our hopes for life and happiness.

But to the Believer God's word is unequivocal. Irrespective of our circumstances we are at all times to trust Him. Furthermore He makes it plain we will not please Him otherwise; *"but my righteous one shall live by faith; And if he shrinks back my soul has no pleasure in him"* (Hebrews 10:38). God does not say it is hard to please Him without faith, He says it is impossible. Whatever touches our life, God expects us to respond with faith. There are no exceptions, there are no excuses; everyone of us is to trust God at all times, in all situations. Yet how can a person go on believing in God with the same deep trust, when His Word has not held up in our life?

If we want to see the meaning of a particular word or phrase, a good rule is to find the first instance of it's use in the Bible. The young basketball star who quoted 'the righteous live by faith' most likely read these words in the New Testament, either in the book of Hebrews or Romans. He may be surprised to know that in both instances the writers are using a quotation from the Old Testament. Our young basketball star would be even more surprised to discover the circumstances under which these words were spoken by God. It wasn't to a winner; this famous phrase was spoken to the prophet Habakkuk facing the severest setback to his faith.

Here are the circumstances: the nation of Judah had become apostate, wickedness prevailed over righteousness. Justice came out perverted, strife and contention marked everyday life. Dismayed at the corruption and violence, Habakkuk called out to God, "How long God, will you put up with this? Why do you not do something?" God responded with an answer that completely staggered Habakkuk. He was raising up the Chaldean's to invade and conquer Israel. This dreaded ungodly nation who worshipped their own strength were absolutely without mercy and no one could stand against them. They had an insatiable appetite for violence, sweeping through and devastating the land they conquered, mocking those they subjugated, taking off captives and booty.

Habakkuk knew Israel was deserving of God's punishment, but questioned how a holy God could use an evil nation as His instrument. After all, Israel was God's chosen people, distinguished from all other nations by God's favor. They were under His protection. It is by saving His people God shows forth his glory to other peoples. As a light to all the nations, Israel has a divine destiny to fulfill in God's redemptive purpose toward the rest of mankind. Israel, the land God promised to Abraham and his descendants forever. The perpetuation of this nation state is essential. How can God let them die? You can imagine Habakkuk's agitation, the whole premise and foundation of his understanding of God is undermined. Surely God must act to stop this genocide in which women and children will be slaughtered.

True faith begins where the atheist thinks it should leave off.

The problem for the prophet is the same as for the Jewish writer who cannot fathom God's inactivity in the holocaust. "How can God look on evil?" Unable to reconcile these contradictions, Habakkuk sought enlightenment. God responded, but not with the explanation Habakkuk sought. He told the prophet to write the prophesy down in large letters and post it where everyone could read it. On the heels of this instruction God utters the famous phrase, "but the righteous will live by his faith" (Habakkuk 2:4). When we read this Mount Everest of faith scripture our understanding of the quality of faith God calls us to is shaped by the context in which it is spoken. Habakkuk has heard what he believes is the death knell for His nation and God is going to do nothing to prevent the tragedy. Indeed God is behind the catastrophic events that will unfold. True faith begins where the atheist thinks it should leave off. That is to say, when all of our understanding of God is shattered and He acts as an agent of destruction instead of a savior. When God's behavior is at odds with our understanding of who He is, true faith looks to the future and anticipates in spite of everything, God will be true to His Word.

The prophet Habakkuk who initially rebelled against God by declaring, "You cannot do that," responded to the challenge and was by the end of the book praising God and declaring he would wait patiently for the unfolding of events. The final verses express a sublime faith: *"Though the fig tree should not blossom, And there be no fruit on the vines, Though the yield of the olive should fail, And the fields produce no food, Though the flock should be cut off from the fold, And there be no cattle in the stalls, Yet I will exult in the LORD, I will rejoice in the God of my salvation" (Habakkuk 3:17,18).* All that makes for life and ordered existence may be falling apart around the prophet, every evidence may be that God's order is disintegrating, yet Habakkuk will trust God to save His people! This is either stupidity, the sort that goes back to stand on a rug after it has been pulled out from under you once, or it is audacious faith.

Audacious Faith

chapter eleven

Numerous Christian books have been written to explain suffering. Various thoughts are suggested:

God sees our heartache and takes our loss seriously...
God has purposes that we cannot understand....
We are part of a fallen human race, we live in an imperfect world...
God's ways are above our ways...

None of these observations alleviate the real pain for someone who has expressed their life in terms of Gods' favor and blessing. Not only is there no meaningful future to look forward to, but the precepts by which they ordered their life and the canon they have considered axiomatic have been undermined leaving them not only without hope, but also without a testimony.

Before I get too excited about Habakkuk's faith I need to know whether it springs from hope. After all, faith is the assurance of things hoped for. The second thing I am curious about is how his faith reconciles God's inaction in the face of evil. Habakkuk's complaint after all was that a Savior could not stand by while evil triumphed over His people. The credibility of Habakkuk's faith is in question here. Is it an expression of heartfelt admiration for God, or does it have more in common with the behavior of a battered spouse who, lacking the character or will to leave her husband, instead defends his abusive behavior? Assuming Habakkuk's faith is genuine, then the question arises how did he arrive at this faith? It is this last question I want to look at first - the 'how' of this faith before discussing the validity of it, and to do so I am going to use a salesmen as an analogy.

Jesus did not hesitate to use unbelievers as an example if they showed more wisdom than Believers. Christians can learn a lot about dealing with disappointment by observing how salesmen go about maintaining a positive attitude. Commission salesmen face more rejection in the course of their job than those in any other vocation, especially those who do cold calling door to door. The enthusiasm is there when they begin their day, but by the end of a day of having doors closed firmly in their faces and without a sale, their spirits flag. Out of necessity, then, salesmen have had to learn to handle disappointment.

How do salesmen bounce back when setbacks are so much a part of their daily lot? They go to 'the word' - no not the Bible, but a whole genre of success books with such titles as "See You At The Top," "Think and Grow Rich", "How To Negotiate What You Want", "Winning At Life". They read these books because they give them the keys for successful selling. They also attend conferences and listen to motivational speakers tell them, "You can be anything you want to be, no other job in the world lets you set your own income level." They listen avidly as the speakers emphasize the rewards of successful selling - a million dollar dream home, a yacht, a new car every year, exotic vacations - and the lifestyle they always imagined as out of reach suddenly becomes attainable. These high powered apostles of success not only raise the expectation level in their audience, they also generate a belief in ones self. They use phrases like "the hidden power within", "unleashing your true potential". They emphasize attitude... "it all has to do with your attitude ..... attitude equals altitude ... you can soar to undreamed of heights with the right attitude." The salesmen who attend soak it up and come away from the meetings convinced there is nothing beyond their reach, no limitations to what they can accomplish except the limitations they place on themselves. There is a lot in common between these conferences and a good old fiery revival meeting where the congregation comes out all fired up and ready to go out and win the world for Christ.

The symbols are obvious; the word, faith and hope. The same symbols that inspire Christians. Although the 'word' in this instance is not the Bible, and their hope is usually materialistic, and the faith they generate is based upon attitude, not God.

What is the lesson here? Just this; salesmen (or their company) willingly part with hundreds, even thousands of dollars to attend these conferences. They place a high value upon attitude as being the key to success in life. More importantly, the great truth salesmen have learned is that the word is the best counter to a setback. They re-read the same success books and listen over and over to old audio tapes in the car between calls, messages they already know by heart, because they know the only way to counter a setback is to feed their mind with positive images. The word neutralizes the failure by reviving faith and hope. Faith and hope are going to get us through adversity. Nothing revives tired feet like reminding yourself why you are working and the reward that comes with success. When you have had a bad week and feel discouraged because you have made no sales and attend the weekly sales team meeting and hear another sales person's story of a big sale it inspires you to get back out and try again. When you have just lost a sale and feel discouraged, you pop another tape in the tape deck and your favorite motivational guru says, 'it is not so bad as it looks. It is only a setback. A few doors down the road there is a big sale that will give you a month's worth of commission.' So salesmen keep the word close at hand; its message ever fresh in their mind, ready to put the next rejection in perspective. This is not the end, only a setback.

Many Christians have not prepared themselves for disappointment; they aren't expecting setbacks because deep down they have a mentality that says "bad things don't happen to Christians." In the church today are groups who have emphasized the theology of blessing to such an extent they have ruled out any adversity and suffering altogether. They are variously described by the terms 'prosperity gospel,' a 'theology of glory,' 'name it and claim it' teachings. When things go wrong, those who think of Jesus as someone who will keep them from hardship and distress are taken off guard. Typically their response is to do the very thing they ought not, the worst possible thing; they let go of the Lord's hand. Their church attendance drops, eventually stopping altogether; they stop praying, they stop reading the Bible. All the things that normally act to bring the word of God into their lives they cease. In their grief they wrestle alone trying to come to terms with their dilema. "I don't understand, I prayed, I fasted. I really believed God was in this." A big "why?" casts its' shadow over their lives.

So long as you remain preoccupied with the "why?" of disappointment, your focus is in the wrong place for overcoming adversity - in the past. A friend of mine was part of a church that broke up. Some have never returned to be part of a church and my friend says when he has run into them on occasion over the years, they immediately begin to discuss the circumstances under which they broke up trying to understand how it could have happened. Because the 'Why God?" remains unanswered they have never gone on with the Lord. They have never come to terms with their disappointment, and consequently they've never gotten beyond tragedy.

Obviously if we are committed in an enterprise we don't just shrug it off and move on to new things overnight. Plainly a setback will make us depressed, even despondent, depending upon how emotionally involved we were in the venture. In our grief we may tell ourselves there is nothing to live for and go to bed at night not wanting to wake up in the morning. There is no need to reproach ourselves for feeling down, but obviously if we do not take steps to overcome these feelings the tragedy will overcome us. Salesmen realize how important it is to put a setback behind them, so they don't waste time dwelling on questions that may have no answers. They keep failure in perspective. "I don't understand why I missed the sale, however I did and I accept it. It is not the end, only a setback on the road to success." Salesmen overcome setbacks because they have factored them into life. Unfortunately, many Christians haven't. Bad things do happen to Christians. Only when they accept the fact that an omniscient God foresaw the disappointment and did nothing to prevent it, will they be able to make the leap of faith that while there are failures there are never hopeless situations.

Get back to worship.

Once he heard God's exhortation for faith Habakkuk immediately ceased to ask God for an explanation. Regardless of the apparent contradiction between God's actions and His promises, and despite whatever inner conflict and tensions he felt, Habakkuk worshipped God. I imagine initially he might have been feeling numb and bewildered. It is likely his praises may not have been very enthusiastic and probably his professions of faith did not carry a whole lot of conviction, but instinctively Habakkuk knew enough not to separate himself from the people of God. When our faith takes a blow it is imperative as a first and necessary step toward recovery we do not cease our practice of worship, for if we do we shut ourselves off from the Word of God.

As we read on we see Habakkuk's worship takes the form of a review of God's history with the nation, in particular God's acts of deliverance of Israel in the past. The ground trembles, the mountains quake as God's avenging wrath is directed against Israel's enemies. Habakkuk praises a warrior-God indignantly marching through the earth angrily trampling the nations for the salvation of Israel. God deliberately took aim with his bow and shot His arrows for Israel. The sun and moon stood still while God went to the help of Israel. Habakkuk repeats all these reports as praise. Do you see what he is doing? He is reviewing reports of God's mighty protection of the nation in the past and from this he became convinced that God would act to save Israel in the future, in spite of the fact that His present actions appeared to be to the contrary. When God is silent and seems far from helping we are most likely to question His care and willingness to save. Remembering God's help in the past restores our trust in Gods character, as the psalmist who penned the following words testifies:

"Then I said, "It is my grief, That the right hand of the Most High has changed.

I shall remember the deeds of the LORD; Surely I will remember Thy wonders of old" (Psalm 77:10,11).

Faith is not blind.

This is a key point. Faith is not flight from reality, nor is it blind. It is not a refusal to look at the evidence and denial of truth as so many critics say. Habakkuk looks squarely at the impending calamity, he knows it will not be averted, but at the same time he looks back into the past to see that the violence Israel suffered was not chaotic and unrestrained. God was in control and He took action to save His people. Those who do not go to church do not sense God's nearness in times of disaster. It is little wonder they cannot get past the question "Where was God?" Faith does not try to answer the question "Why God?" Instead faith says, "God is my King and Deliverer, He was so in the past, He will be so now and in the future."

Christians need to take a leaf out of the salesman's manual, and in the same way put failure behind them and inspire themselves with the Word. "I can do all things through Christ who strengthens me... if Christ be for us, who can be against us... the steps of a good man are ordered by the Lord, though he fall he shall not be cast down." These and many other promises remind the Christian in the midst of sorrow and despondency that their troubles are under God's control, things have not gotten out of hand. "In all things" - yes, all things, no matter how bad they seem - "God works for the good of those who love Him." The Word of God promises every believer that there is no cause for despair, since out of the deepest tragedies of life a creative God can work good. The future is not bleak. No matter how grim the outlook is, hope thou in God. Do what salesmen would do - write these promises out and put them on the refrigerator, the dashboard of your car, wherever they can be seen, say them out loud, get up and stomp around the house saying them over and over, put them on tape and play them back to youself in the car; anything to impress them into the subconscious of your mind.

Some Christians scornfully dismiss this with the offhand remark, "That positive confession upbeat stuff does nothing for me." *They are wrong.* If we are to overtake our disappointment then the paramount need is to change our feelings. Depression is a feeling. It is a manifestation of doubt and unbelief which if not checked becomes despondency and undermines any incentive to go on. We need to recapture our feeling of enthusiasm, a word described by one motivational author as "God within us." Enthusiasm needs to be nourished. It is not self sustaining. The Bible itself makes it clear we are to take the initiative in this regard:

> *Why are you in despair, O my soul? And why have you become disturbed within me? Hope in God, for I shall yet praise Him, The help of my countenance, and my God (Psalm 42:11).*
>
> *In everything give thanks; for this is God's will for you in Christ Jesus (1 Thessalonians 5:18).*

Praise Him in all circumstances, give thanks in all circumstances. Do not wait until you feel like praising Him. Feelings change as you work at changing them. Praise comes as you open your mouth and force yourself to praise. Ask the Holy Spirit to lift you up in the inner man, tell Him you are empty and ask for the holy fire of the Spirit of God to fall on you afresh.

Praising God when I am down has nothing to do with pretense. It has everything to do with feelings and how to go about changing them. By reminding myself of God's precious promises, His love and care, I'm taking the focus away from my immediate pain which is causing me doubt and unbelief, and focusing on an end which is encouraging and hopeful. By allowing the end to determine my feelings, I'm making a selection as to what shall influence my mood. By engaging the Word of God I'm telling myself that no matter what is going on now God is in control. In this way I serve to encourage myself. I renew my enthusiasm, engendering optimism.

To the skeptic who claims self-help slogans are a set-up for disappointment, we need to make the distinction between a quick fix and persistence. Slogans are intended to keep salesmen on track, with the guarantee that ultimately success will come. For the doubting salesman who says, "How can you guarantee success? I just flat out can't sell. I went out all last week and sold nothing. I am never going to sell anything. That positive thinking stuff may work for you but not me," experienced salesmen have an answer. The conviction that they will succeed and make sales is locked into a reality. They have a formula which goes something like this, "For every fifteen cold calls I make I will get six prospects. For every six prospects I will get five interviews. For every five interviews I will close on two and make the sale." So long as he is doing all the basics properly at each stage of selling - prospecting for customers, approaching them, interviewing, and finally closing the sale - then that formula will hold true. When the salesman is going through a bad patch, that formula encourages him because he knows it has proven accurate in the past. The formula guarantees in time his sales figures will pick up and he will make his sales targets. So the salesman looks at his goals and the formula reassures him his goals are still achievable, despite any reverses he may presently be experiencing.

In the same way the man of faith believes God stands behind His Word. Therefore whatever his circumstances may say to the contrary, God will be true to his Word. God is not a liar. He never spoke a word in vain. He never made a promise he could not keep.

A credible faith.

Now that we have looked at the steps Habakkuk took to revive his faith we need to turn our attention to the credibility of that faith. As Habakkuk continues to worship he gets an insight into God's ways. Apparently God can use even those such as the Chaldeans who are hardened in their opposition toward Him to further his purposes. This is the answer to the question of the holocaust, and to the pastor's wife whose husband left her for another woman. This is the answer to the sign on the card at the murdered child's funeral, 'Why God?' God will allow evil to befall His people. This is not a popular notion, it is one that many Christians do not want to believe. If we think God will keep us from suffering at the hands of evildoers we are mistaken. Jesus rebuts that notion when he said His followers would be persecuted. The Lord's prayer does not seek to be kept from evil but delivered from evil. It is an important and significant distinction. In the words of author F.B. Meyer,

> *"The evil thing may originate in the malignity of a Judas; but by the time it reaches us, it has become the cup which our Father has given us to drink. The waster may purpose his own lawless and destructive work; but he cannot go an inch beyond the determinate counsel and foreknowledge of God. Satan himself must ask permission before he touches a hair of the*

patriarch's head. The point up to which we may be tested is fixed by consummate wisdom. The weapon may hurt and the fire sting; but they are in the hands which redeemed us. Nothing can fall on us without God's permission, and His permissions are our appointments. We cannot be the sport of blind fate or chance; for in trial we are still in the hands of the Divine savior."

The idea that God can be behind catastrophic events is not one many Christians are willing to face. But we should qualify this with an important observation: God is not evil! The actions of Judas in betraying Jesus were those of a wicked man, but at the same time it was the will of God that Jesus should die on the cross. The evil in Judas actions cannot be traced back to God, any more than the actions of a child murderer or the atrocities of Nazi Germany can be attributed to God. God punishes evil: He does not condone it, and though the Chaldean's are permitted to vanquish Israel, they would not escape punishment for their deeds. Those very same nations they vanquished would dispense Gods retribution. There is justice. We live in a world in which God allows human evil to win at times. Living under the momentary triumph of evil, we raise serious questions concerning justice and wait for God to answer. Though it may seem in the short term that wickedness pays, and it makes no difference whether one keeps God's law or not, in the end there will be a reckoning. If that day of reckoning seems inordinately slow in coming, yet the faithful wait for it.

Habakkuk looks ahead in fear and trembling to the terrible day of the Lord that lies ahead for his people, knowing it will not be averted and yet at the same time with confidence and full of faith, for the future he sees is

*F.B. Meyer, Tried By Fire, CLC Publications, Fort Washington, PA., 28,29. Used by permission.

full of the glory of the Lord in which righteousness and justice prevail. It is a future to look forward to. God's actions have not compromised His character. He is opposed to evil, He has been true to His word, He has perpetuated the nation of Israel. God has been able to bring about a good future, one in which justice flows like a river. Habakkuk's faith in God was sustained upon the grounds that God's declared purposes for Israel had not changed.

From Tragedy to Triumph

chapter twelve

'For I know the plans that I have for you,' declares the LORD, 'plans for welfare and not for calamity to give you a future and a hope'.
(Jeremiah 29:11)

God has promised us a meaningful future. This is our grounds for optimism whatever failures and sorrows may come into our life. We cannot be victims of chance or fate since God's plan for our life was established while we were yet unborn. When the tragic and unexpected come into our life it is good to know an omniscient God foresaw the event when He settled upon His purposes over our life. He is not scrambling like some master strategist to come up with an alternative plan. Paul had insight into this when he declared ".. we know that God causes all things to work together for good to those who love God, to those who are called according to His purpose" (Romans 8:28).

By faith Abraham, when tested was prepared to offer up Isaac of whom God had said, "through Isaac shall your descendents be named." The promises of God were bound up in the survival of Isaac, yet unhesitatingly Abraham prepared to slay his son, confident that God would reconcile his hope for a posterity with the command to slay his son. This is why Abraham's faith is so remarkable, and why Abraham is known as the father of the faith whose descendants we are. Nothing can ever touch our lives that will rob us of our hope. God will never require of us that we settle for second best. He will not substitute misery and deprivation for joy and fullness and call that desirable. For those who hope in God there is a future, and the future is good. What makes it possible is our faith!

Emmaus road.

On the eve of His crucifixion Jesus, knowing the end was near, told His disciples, "You will be sorrowful, but your sorrow will be turned to joy." Only Jesus had the faith to see that the same crisis that made for sorrow would be the cause for great joy. In a wonderfully touching story the Bible relates how this happened for two of Jesus' disciples. Making their sorrowful way home to Emmaus after the Passover these disillusioned disciples are discussing the tragic events, trying to make sense of things. At some point along the road Jesus comes alongside and begins to walk with them, though they fail to recognize Him. When Jesus asks them about their conversation they relate to Him the crucifixion events concluding with the lament, "We were hoping that it was He who was going to redeem Israel" The Bible tells us that beginning with Moses and with all the prophets Jesus explained to them the things concerning Himself in all the Scriptures and in particular why it was necessary for the Christ to suffer before entering his glory.

These two men had a hope for a Messiah, but one who was a warrior conqueror. Jesus showed them from scripture that the Messiah was a suffering servant. Their savior was a political king who would protect the borders of Israel. The scope and magnitude of God's plan of salvation went beyond political stability to eternal security. These men hoped for freedom from their Roman conquerors; God gave them freedom from the power of sin. These men's messianic hope was limited to a deliverer for Israel; God's plan went beyond Israel to save all the nations. Sometimes it is necessary for us to be disillusioned before God can bring forth his greater glory. Until our presumptions are discredited we are neither open nor amenable to God's point of view. As these two chastened men listen to Jesus they hear an explanation to their questions that squares with events and they are forced toward new considerations. "Were not our hearts burning within us?" they remarked later. This is a metaphor of hope breaking in anew. In the climax to the story the little group finally reaches Emmaus, home to the two disciples, and they invite Jesus in to eat with them. In the act of breaking bread they recognize Him, and Jesus vanishes from sight.

When Jesus died on the cross so did the hopes of these two men for a Messiah. Their hope had to be quickened. Once it was, their eyes were opened to see the messiah they hoped for right beside them. Oh this is too wonderful, I get goose bumps just thinking about it. That Passover weekend was the climax of God's plan of salvation and the cornerstone was a resurrected Jesus. Jesus' death which they saw as the end, was just the beginning of God's plan for the lives of these two men.

Emmaus road starts out with those disillusioned words, "we thought." Our basketball star thought God would help him win the championship, but he lost. Our pastors wife never envisioned her husband running off with another woman. She thought they would be a team and grow old serving God. Jan and I thought the trip to America would be a stepping stone to some sort of Christian service. We thought something might work out for us to stay in America. Instead we found ourselves back in New Zealand broke, looking for a job and a place to live. I had borrowed money for our airfares home, I borrowed more to buy a car, and suddenly I was deeply in debt. The trip to America felt like I had taken a turn on a merry-go-round and been spun off exactly where I was before I got on. Discouraged, I asked myself, "What was that all about?"

Jan got a job but I was unable to find regular work. The economy was still very depressed and all I could get was some part-time occasional work on building sites. Work I hated. We didn't make enough even to live on. I put an advertisement in the newspaper for a place to rent that would allow me to work off the rent. We got a house owned by an orthodontist who used part of the premises to conduct his business. We had to be out of the house during business hours when the orthodontist was working. He had it by day, we had it by night and even then we had to share the facilities with the orthodontist's son who had a basement room. It was a place to sleep, that was all. Every penny we earned went to paying back what we owed. Those were hard times. I remember wet, cold winter days when I could get no work and had to sit in the car because I had to fill in time waiting for evening when the orthodontist would be finished with his work before I could go home. I was so poor I had no money even to buy a coffee or sandwich. I was thirty five, broke, and without a trade. Prospects for a good paying job, one I would like, were slim to nothing. The last few years had led me nowhere but back to where I started. I thought about taking an adult apprenticeship. I wondered if I should go back to school and learn some vocation. And then I thought, "Heck, what would I do? All I want to do is to serve God."

I was so frustrated, so demoralized. I felt like I had wasted the past few years of my life, and what was worse I couldn't see a future to look forward to. Things just seemed to get harder and harder. At some point not long after our return to New Zealand Jan got pregnant but miscarried. Nothing was going right for us. I remember one time sitting in the car, on a wet miserable day, in tune with my mood. I had finished reading the situations vacant column of the newspaper- an exercise in despair, looking at jobs none of which roused the least bit of interest. I was utterly without a purpose, just an absolute lack of fulfillment in my life. I hit the steering wheel in frustration and swore. I might have been swearing at God. I know I was angry with God.

"You are a big disappointment to me God!"

You lead me on. You let me think I am special and you have a purpose for my life.

I am no different from anyone else."

Gradually Jan and I picked up our lives back in New Zealand. Our first son was born a couple of years later and I was excelling in a new career with great prospects. We attended a large church of which I was a deacon. I enjoyed church, the worship was uplifting. The preaching was good and though my desire to serve God remained largely unfulfilled, I felt good in myself, positive and optimistic. I had begun to study the Word again and to do some writing. Writing seemed to be the one positive thing that had come out of our time in the USA. I found I had a talent for it, and I enjoyed it. We were getting on with life. Then without warning I suddenly became dissatisfied with church. For some reason the worship, once so full of the presence of the Lord, seemed flat and empty. The preaching didn't seem to stimulate me as it used to, I was bored with church and had to make myself go. When I went I was restless and came away empty. I thought at first it was just me, I just needed to give it time and it would pass. It didn't, and I found myself to my consternation feeling increasingly out of place in church. I had a problem with my attitude and no matter how hard I tried I couldn't shake it. After some months had gone by I couldn't see anything else to do but confess it to the pastor. With some trepidation I made an appointment to see him and tell him his church was boring me. I could imagine how this implied criticism of himself as pastor would go down, but I really felt I hadn't any choice.

Hope breaking in anew.

When I had finished telling him how I felt, he said very simply and calmly, "Ken, my wife and I were discussing you and Jan the other day. You don't belong here. You need to go back to the USA. You got spoiled there. It is where God wants you." It was a word from God and the words brought tears to my eyes. More than anything I still wanted to serve God but I had put it out of my mind. God still wanted me. He wanted me to return to America. I blinked back tears. I had put aside any thought of returning to America, yet deep down it was still a desire. And in that moment the desire returned like a flood and more than anything I wanted to go back to America. Suddenly my mind was racing. God has a purpose for my life. He took us to America for a reason. The future is in America, just as we thought. I was also right in thinking he had future purposes for us there. But I had imposed my timetable upon God and in my presumption erred. I was getting confirmation that God had a purpose for our life, and along with it new insight and understanding. It was as if God was saying, "Though my plans for you have tarried, yet prepare to go back to America, for my plans for you hasten toward their goal."

I was so excited when I left the pastor, I can't remember one thing he said once I heard 'USA.' Like the disciples on the Emmaus road the word of God was coming to me in a way that rekindled my hopes. I didn't know what to make of it right then, but I tell you my heart was burning. Go back to the USA, but how? To live in the USA we would need to work to support ourselves and for that you need a special visa - what is commonly called a green card. There are a number of categories with quotas under which one may apply. Political refugee's can get special visas. Professional sportsmen can get visas to play and live in the USA. Entrepreneurs with investment capital and workers with special skills in demand can get visas. Your status and how many are applying determines the likelihood of getting a visa. Without a special category you are at the bottom of the ladder and rumor was it took years to get a visa. Someone told us about a religious category under which you could apply for a visa, and upon research we discovered we qualified. You did not need be an ordained minister; the only stipulation to qualify was you had to have been at least two years in a leadership position in your church. As a deacon I qualified to apply for a religious visa. I liked that, it satisfied my sense of propriety. God was sending us, we were going to serve Him. What was more fitting, then, than to apply for a visa on the grounds that established the purpose for our visa application.

There remained one other hurdle. To qualify for a religious visa a church in the USA had to sponsor us. When we were travelling down the interstate five from Vancouver to Seattle after being refused entry into Canada, we were devastated. God had failed us. Fortunately Art and Mary took charge. They made a call ahead to the fellowship we had previously visited, who agreed to put us up until we could sort things out and make arrangements to get home. Dan and Jeannie, whom we had previously stayed with, were glad to have us back. Dan and Jeannie had the gift of hospitality, the rare ability to put people at ease, they made it seem as if we had done them a favor by inconveniencing them. We made arrangements with family to purchase a ticket for us to get home and while we waited for the ticket to arrive, we spent about a week in Washington where we got to know and love the people in the small fellowship in whose midst we found ourselves. Our hearts knitted with these people and when we left everyone seemed like old friends. Back in New Zealand we kept in touch by letter. It was this church that sponsored us back into the USA. Our calamity was God's provision for our return.

If the Emmaus Road starts out with a cross and two disillusioned men who had seen their hopes crushed, the journey ends gloriously in the fulfillment of that very same hope. Faith is the only possible response to the tragic and unexpected in life that opens up the future. Some of us have been down the Emmaus road and can look back on some painful lessons in life and say, "That turned out OK." Yes, it was hard at the time, but things worked out for the best. Jan and I got our visa and made it back to the USA. We have made our home here and as I write this have been fourteen years in the USA serving the Lord. I have found my gifting in writing and the opportunity to pursue that here in America.

So What

chapter thirteen

> *As to this salvation, the prophets who prophesied of the grace that would come to you made careful search and inquiry.*
> **(1 Peter 1:10)**

It is sometimes thought that the authors of scripture simply sat down and wrote as God put the words in their minds. The inference is that the authors themselves had nothing to do with God's revelation, they were just the instruments God used to put pen to paper. This scripture proves otherwise. It shows that the prophets were inspired in regard to their visions and revelations because they were inquiring of God about the matters of which they wrote. The great truth revealed here is that revelation from God is preceded by the searching mind of man. Two different terms, 'search' and 'inquiry,' are used to indicate the intensity of thought and examination these writers brought to their reading of scripture. The authors of scripture had a great curiosity about God's word and in response God revealed things to them that would otherwise have remained unknown. The prophet Daniel is an example; he read a prophecy a former prophet, Jeremiah, had made in regard to Israel's devastation and it prompted him to pray to the Lord on behalf of the nation. He tells how he went about it, *"So I gave my attention to the Lord God to seek Him by prayer and supplications, with fasting, sackcloth, and ashes" (Daniel 9:3)*. Now that is serious inquiry, wouldn't you say? In response to Daniel's prayer for understanding the angel Gabriel came and said, *"O Daniel, I have now come forth to give you insight with understanding" (Daniel 9:22)*.

The real need amongst so many Christians is not to commit more scriptures to memory, but to get insight with understanding of the scriptures they already know. Many in the church would be hard pressed if they had to give an explanation of the basic tenets of the faith, the relevant verses which they can readily recite by memory. Spurgeon, the nineteenth century preacher, tells the story of a church member who when asked what he believed said, "I believe what the church believes."

"What does the church believe" he was asked?

"The church believes what I believe."

"And pray what do you and the church believe?"

"Why we believe the same thing" the man replied.

As Spurgeon concluded, it is idle for a man to say 'I am a Believer' and not know what he believes.

You can be industrious yet poor, and this is especially true when it comes to reading the word of God. At one time or another in church we have heard a person untrained in public speaking reading aloud from the Bible in the same dull monotone throughout the passage without any inflexion in the voice at all, running the words together, eager to finish and sit down. We bring that same mentality into our private devotions. Concerned only to get in our

So What

allocated scripture reading for the day and be done, we rush over the verses barely thinking about what the words have to say. We are not drawing anything from the text in front of us because we are not pressing it with questions.

I once sold Massey Ferguson tractors, and part of my on-the-job training was to attend a product knowledge seminar run by a company 'expert' sent out from England. I had been around farms most of my life and thought I knew all about tractors. Short of announcing a price drop for MF tractors which farmers kept reminding us were higher than the opposition, I didn't see how the 'expert' was going to help us sell more tractors. My low expectations seemed to be borne out when I arrived at the first meeting and saw beside each seat the product brochures listing the specifications for the different tractors we sold. "We are going to sit here all day and read brochures? How boring this is going to be" I mused. Then the 'expert' entered the room and began going over the specs, but as he did he asked the question, "So what?"

"So the tractor has an oil capacity of 11 gallons, so what?"

"So the maximum torque is at 1300 rpm, so what?"

He made us go through all the specs each time asking us the question, "so what?"

I found out my knowledge of tractors was much less than I thought.

He explained the significance of each spec and then he compared them with the opposition tractors whose brochures he handed out. The opposition tractor was cheaper, yes, but it had a lower oil capacity, not enough to make a turn using power steering while operating a hydraulic implement. They had to mount an unsightly reserve oil tank at extra cost if they wanted to run a potato harvester. The opposition tractor was rated at 50 horse power, three more than our most popular model. But wait a minute, where was it rated, at the power take off like ours, or the engine where it will be higher? The only significant rating so far as the farmer is concerned is the horsepower available at the PTO. The opposition rated theirs at the engine, it was in fact less than ours at the PTO. Those spec sheets I had never taken much notice of highlighted the features of our tractor, revealing its advantages over the opposition in a way I had never seen before. I came away from the seminar persuaded that not only did we have the best tractor, but it was also the best value. I have never forgotten that lesson. When you read something, ask the question, "So what?" The specs are there for a reason, whether a tractor has 7 or 11 gallons of oil has a significance, or whether maximum torque is developed at 1300rpm or 1800rpm has a benefit or disadvantage to the farmer. If he is unaware of the significance he is not going to make a sound decision in the purchase of a tractor.

The Bible can be like the spec sheets of a tractor were to me prior to the seminar, familiar, yet their significance little understood and therefore lacking any inspirational power. Far too many in the church treat scripture as little more than a collection of wise sayings offering applied psychology and self improvement. The Bible is not appreciated for anything more than good advice on how to get by in life: If you are sad read Psalm so and so, if you are in doubt read this verse, if you are anxious here is a verse for you, if you need encouragement read another verse, and so on, and so on. They have never seen the Bible in terms of God's grand plan of salvation and that from start to finish there is an interconnectedness and unity. Instead of committing to read a certain number of chapters of the Bible each day, we would be better off to read less, employing a concordance and commentary to better understand the scriptures we already know by rote.

I have heard people express the sentiment that they take the word of God at face value, implying that study is unnecessary and unduly complicates a simple word. The trouble with taking scriptures at face value is that they sometimes contradict one another. Jesus said, *"Do not judge lest you be judged yourselves"(Matthew 7:1).* Was He saying, that we should never be critical of other people? Certainly there are some Christians who think we should never entertain a negative thought about someone else. Well, if this is so what did Jesus mean when He said, *"Be on your guard! If your brother sins, rebuke him; and if he repents, forgive him" (Luke 17:3).* How can you rebuke someone unless you have first passed judgement on their behavior? Obviously those two scriptures need to be studied if they are to be reconciled.

Take as another example Paul's teaching to the Jews that they need not circumcise their children or follow the customs of their fathers in order to be justified in God's sight. Yet in Acts we read when he arrived in Jerusalem, at the suggestion of the apostles, he purified himself along with four men according to Jewish law as a public demonstration that he himself did walk orderly, keeping the Law (Acts 21:21). Why would Paul do that if it were not necessary, and especially in light of his actions when he publicly rebuked the apostle Peter for following Jewish tradition in eating apart from the Gentiles. Taken at face value these scriptures lead to the inevitable conclusion that the apostle Paul was inconsistent. Clearly the Bible needs to be studied.

The increased knowledge I got out of the tractor seminar had an immediate impact. It increased my confidence and enthusiasm for selling. I was a far more effective communicator and as a result I was more successful. Farmers aren't very interested in listening to a salesman quoting specs for a tractor, especially when the farmer has a shed full of Ford tractors or John Deere's, and the salesman is from Massey Ferguson. But they listen carefully to someone who can tell them what the specs mean and how it can benefit them. Similarly the world is turned off by Christian cliches, but when God's point of view is presented with insightful sound reasoning they cannot ignore it.

Once to make some extra money I hired out to mow lawns. I got a job helping a retired psychology professor with his yard work. At the time I was writing a Christian column which appeared each week in the local paper. For several days I worked alongside the professor, an engaging and interesting person to talk to, although I could tell from our discussions he was not a man of faith. One day he said to me, "Your name sounds familiar." I sometimes got this upon meeting people for the first time, usually it was because they were familiar with my name through the newspaper. I told him I wrote a column in the newspaper, perhaps he had seen my name there. "What column" he asked? "The Living Word" I replied and waited for his reaction. He looked hard at me before replying, "I read it every week. I don't believe a word you say." He paused for a moment before adding , "but I like the way you say it."

I think that is the best complement I have ever had to my writing. Any communicator covets the attention of his or her audience, perhaps even above persuading them to their point of view. To present the word of God to an unbeliever in such a way that they are forced to consider it and take note is the object of all Christian communication. They might not like or agree with what is being said, but they cannot dismiss it as another Christian cliche because it is compelling with a wisdom that confounds their own. The professor told me he had had Christian students in his classes over the years but had a very low opinion of them because whenever they used scripture in a discussion they could never argue their position. As far as he was concerned they were out of touch with the world, reactionaries holding onto outdated superstitions and prejudices. We need people who can argue Gods point of view in the world because more and more the society we live in today reflects an acceptance of ungodly wisdom and values. Modern day spokespersons of a Christian worldview have done a wonderful job of presenting the Christian view to counter the prevailing worldview. When presented thus it is compelling, and media and legislators alike are forced to take notice.

The word of God is not too hard to comprehend.

There are some in the church who just throw up their hands and say, "These things are too difficult for me, I will leave it to the minister and the theologians that's what they are paid for." I would not deny the Bible can be hard to understand, yet there is no suggestion that some truths are too hard for ordinary people to handle. The Bible does not approve of a blind faith. It is the obligation of every Believer to share the gospel, so we need to think about what we are being taught. This is the point the writer of Hebrews was making to the church; *"For though by this time you ought to be teachers, you have need again for someone to teach you the elementary principles of the oracles of God, and you have come to need milk and not solid food. For everyone who partakes only of milk is not accustomed to the word of righteousness, for he is a babe. But solid food is for the mature, who because of practice have their senses trained to discern good and evil. Therefore leaving the elementary teaching about the Christ, let us press on to maturity, not laying again a foundation of repentance from dead works and of faith toward God" (Hebrews 5:12 - 6:1).*

There were those in the church who had never gotten beyond the basic tenets of the faith. It is as if they were in college taking a class in chemistry and the teacher was still going over the table of elements with them. We would expect from a college student that they would be figuring more things out for themselves and capable of doing advanced experiments, putting to good use the basic knowledge they had been taught in elementary school. The writer admonished these believers for their lack of maturity in the faith. He had more to tell them but couldn't because they were stuck at a salvational level. Paul said the same thing to the church at Corinth; *"And I, brethren, could not speak to you as to spiritual men, but as to men of flesh, as to babes in Christ. I gave you milk to drink, not solid food; for you were not yet able to receive it. Indeed, even now you are not yet able" (1 Cor 3:1,2).*

I should emphasize that there are not two levels of teaching. The gospel is simple and every doctrine which can be wrestled with by theologians can be presented to a child. The same truth in one form is milk to the child and in another form solid food for mature Christians. For instance, we teach justification by faith. To a child this means no more than they must believe in Jesus in order to be saved and go to heaven. They can grasp this truth. However, there are implications to the doctrine of justification by faith that are not easily understood, and some first century Jews argued that if a person was justified by faith as Paul claimed then it followed logically that sin did not matter. So Paul had to write the letter of Romans to deal with these and other objections raised by the Jews that the gospel seemed to contradict the Old Testament. To a mature man of God this is meat, but it is the same truth the child learned.

Now this isn't just of historical interest; this misunderstanding of justification by faith persists to this day. Opponents of Christianity sometimes say, "I could never believe in a religion that makes so little demands upon a person". They have never understood that Christianity demands a standard higher than any other religion. Jesus said a person who even lusts for a woman has committed adultery. He also exhorted His disciples to love their enemies and pray for those who persecuted them. The standard of conduct Jesus set His followers is no less than God's holiness. If there were no provision for failure we would fail utterly, so God attributes to us the righteousness of another, Jesus Christ, who kept the law absolutely and in whom no sin was ever found, in order that when we stumble we are covered. God reckons us good (justifies us by faith) in order to make us good.

Oh, the wisdom of God! It takes your breath away. This is the salvation the prophets who wrote scripture longed to know more about. They got a glimpse of the suffering of God's chosen servant and the glories that would follow for God's people, and they searched scripture praying as they did for enlightenment. The result was that they received the revelation we read today as scripture. And it was not only the prophets; the apostle Peter tells us even angels also longed to look into God's plan of salvation. There is so much more to the word of God than we imagined. It hides as much as it reveals and the Holy Spirit makes known the deep things of God only to those who love the word of God enough to be curious.

Writing a newspaper column for five years presenting biblical principles to a secular audience I found out for myself this relationship between revelation and inquiry. I would begin a column on a Monday based on a verse or an idea and end up working hard all day studying scriptures and reading commentaries and other research material. At the end of the day I had nothing to show for my work except a lot of notes, and a whole lot more questions than when I started out. Well into the week I would have several rough drafts and a lot of crossing out and rephrasing sentences, trying to write something that flowed, connecting the various trains of thought. Then one evening while at work I would get a revelation. An idea might come to mind to juxtapose one line of thinking with a scripture, or maybe just a sentence that connects two trains of thought. In the rearrangement of material there would come a clarity and coherence to my writing that was lacking. I'd grab a pen and write down the revelation to rework when I got home later. I would have my column. The pages of notes and rewrites left over testify to the amount of inquiry and study that produced any insight by which the reader might benefit. Revelation takes a lot of hard work.

The need to study scripture is not just a matter of inclination but of necessity. We are more likely to compromise our beliefs when they are not clearly understood. The letters we know as Hebrews and Corinthians were both written to churches that were falling away from the faith. They had become entangled in sin, as the writer of Hebrews phrased it. The reason was directly attributed to their lack of understanding of the word of God. 'Babes' Paul called the Corinthian church, spiritual babes, for their lack of ability to receive more advanced instruction in the scriptures. And like any immature child they were lacking in discernment, unable to distinguish between right and wrong. Their vulnerability had led them into error. In the case of the Corinthian church they had allowed charismatic and eloquent speakers into a place of leadership, vainglorious men who did not have pure servants hearts, who put their own ambitious interests first. As a result the church was dissolving into squabbling factions. These men had achieved their place of leadership in the church primarily because they represented the highest and noblest aspirations of the Greek cultural milieu of the time. They were orators who were proficient in public discourse and able to reason and persuade using logic and oratorical skills. The apostle Paul by comparison it seems was not such an eloquent speaker and his estimation within the church he had founded suffered. These factious leaders who had taken over the church were dismissing him as a nobody, weighty in his writings perhaps but personally unimpressive and contemptible in his speech.

This is a warning for the church today. If we are not mature in our understanding of God's word we become vulnerable to those influences and values that prevail in society. An author of a book writing about the biblical qualities of a wife received notification from a Christian publisher that the manuscript was acceptable so long as they took a chapter out that dealt with the submission of a wife to her husband. Obviously it was out of sync with the spirit of this age which is vigorously promoting women's rights. It is hard to defend submission as the basis for a wholesome relationship when the western world sees the Afghanistan Taliban regime's oppression of woman as an example of submission. All the same, a Christian publisher's job is to promote the biblical worldview. Once they side with the popular view that submission of women is repressive and dysfunctional then very clearly we are seeing an example within the church of conventional wisdom overturning the wisdom of God.

The church is called to be a light in the world. That light grows dim once the church shapes its theology to accommodate prevailing conventional values. Fewer ministers today are willing to denounce sin and preach about the wrath of God. Our culture is uncomfortable making judgements and reluctant to punish offenders. So preachers careful not to offend anyone's sensibilities are adapting to this new climate of tolerance. The teaching of the church is becoming more inclusive, wide enough so as not to turn people away from the church. The percentage of Americans who profess to believe in God is very high. I think over ninety percent say they pray. But to who? Shockingly there are ministers today who declare that they do not believe there is only one way to God. In this day of pluralism which says every belief is valid so long as it is genuinely held, it is politically incorrect to teach that the path to God is a narrow way. Even though Jesus said of Himself *"I am the way, and the truth, and the life; no one comes to the Father, but through Me (John 14:6).* There are churches and denominations who, not wishing to be accused of proselytizing, have gone so far as to endorse other faiths as equally valid in the eyes of God. Is this any different from the actions of ancient Israel who tolerated the pagan altars to coexist in the high places alongside their own altars. Eventually Israel came to worship the Lord, and the pagan god Baal. For that sin God removed His protection and the people were taken into captivity.

We are living in a time and age when it is truer to say of some churches that they are being influenced by the world instead of influencing the world. It behooves those of us who are in the church to make every effort to test the word being preached from the pulpit against the word of God. There are many philosophies and beliefs that seem very plausible. We are responsible for what we believe, or what

So What

we do not believe. Where our ignorance of scripture stems from a neglect of study and indifference to the word, then our ignorance is culpable, and God will let us be taken in by the deceptive wisdom of the world. There are two ways we can come to church; there's the person who sits arms folded saying to themselves, "Lets hear what the minister has to say on this subject." When they don't like what they are hearing they go down the road to another church where the minister has a point of view more amenable to their own. Such people are not seeking God's righteousness, so much as they are a seal of approval over their lifestyle and values. The Bible describes this person as follows: *"For the time will come when they will not endure sound doctrine; but wanting to have their ears tickled, they will accumulate for themselves teachers in accordance to their own desires"* (2 Timothy 4:3). Because they were not willing to be shaped in their thinking by the word of God, God gives these people over to those who will reinforce their error.

The second way we can come to church is like the Jews at Berea who when they heard the gospel presented in their synagogue, *"received the word with great eagerness, examining the Scriptures daily, to see whether these things were so"* (Acts 17:11). They were not so gullible as to embrace a new teaching unquestioningly, nor did they reject it outright because it did not square with their own ideas and notions. They responded by studying scripture to find out for themselves *whether these thing were so*. The Berean's attitude is one we can all emulate. It can be summed up thus: I need to know what the word of God says. What does God's word say? There is the litmus test all conventional wisdom and every notion that is presented as truth, must pass.

Destination Unknown

chapter fourteen

A store owner I once did some work for told me he never set out to be a shopkeeper. "A lot of small decisions brought me here. It was never a goal of mine. You make the best of your circumstances." Have you ever noticed that the impact of decisions you make in life is sometimes not apparent until you are long past that decision point? It would be the testimony of a great many that they never set out to arrive at their present destination. For better or worse their state of affairs is the result of a series of choices, irrespective of whether or not they had the foresight to appreciate the consequences of each decision. The story of Abraham and his nephew Lot is an example. The two had journeyed together since leaving Ur of the Chaldees and had prospered to such an extent the land could no longer support the combined livestock of the two men. Their herders were fighting over land and water rights, which made it necessary to split up. Abraham told Lot he could have his choice of the land before them; *And Lot lifted up his eyes and saw all the valley of the Jordan, that it was well watered everywhere - this was before the LORD destroyed Sodom and Gomorrah - like the garden of the LORD, like the land of Egypt as you go to Zoar. So Lot chose for himself all the valley of the Jordan; and Lot journeyed eastward. Thus they separated from each other (Genesis 13:10,11).*

Lot picked the rich productive land to the east and went in that direction; Abraham went west. It was a disastrous decision for Lot. Two chapters later we read he is living in Sodom, the city which through the ages has remained a byword for wickedness. Four chapters later God destroys Sodom. Lot is saved but his wife and sons-in-law all perish. The last we hear of Lot, this once wealthy man is ruined, living in a cave where his own daughters, having lost their husbands, conspire to get him drunk in order to become pregnant by him. Lot never set out to make his home in Sodom, yet that was the outcome of his decision the day he and Abraham stood together and surveyed the land before them. Sodom was not a consideration when Lot weighed his decision. He probably was not even thinking of it. Lot saw that the Jordan had good pasture for raising livestock. A sound practical business consideration was the basis for his decision to go east. Never-the-less Sodom lay in the direction Lot chose and is where he ended, to his ruin. Many people today would affirm from their own life experience, that like Lot, they never set out to arrive at their present destination.

A decision.

Life has been described as a journey. Each of us is travelling down a path, and along the way we come to intersections where we must decide which way to turn. Though we weigh our decision carefully and deliberately things don't always work out the way we expected. None of

Destination Unknown 171

us knows what the future holds. Man is not in control of his destiny, as the prophet Jeremiah noted when he said *"I know, O LORD, that a man's way is not in himself; Nor is it in a man who walks to direct his steps" (Jeremiah 10:23).*

There are times when the changing circumstances of life thrust decisions upon us and we find ourselves pondering a decision. Graduation, marriage, career choices, these are all significant crossroads in life and the decision we make is very important. Is life a crapshoot? Some are going to be delighted with the way things turn out, others disappointed? A graduate waiting to receive his or her degree looks around at all the other graduates and knows by the law of averages, a high percentage of fellow students who get married will divorce. Others will fail at business ventures, some will make career choices that do not work out, with a future in a dead end job they will hate. A cynic contemplating the future they are faced with says, "Maybe I will be around in fifteen years, but what condition will I be in? Will I end up congratulating myself for the decision I make here today, or will I be making the best of a bad deal?"

At these crossroads in our lives the will of God is important. Is the will of God something planned ahead? If it is and God does indeed have a plan for our life what happens if we make the wrong choice? Will we be lost to the purposes of God in the future? Knowing the will of God is important if we are to make the right choice. Christians pondering their decision seek enlightenment from above. "What is your will, God?" we ask. The answer we seek is the reassurance that we will make the right decision and prosper. I have sometimes found in these situations when I felt I have really needed to hear from God, He has remained silent. Before too long in your walk you will discover that sometimes the guidance you need from God is not forthcoming. You have prayed and God is silent. Then perhaps you feel some anxiety because you cannot give an answer when asked what is God saying to you. We do not always hear God when faced with decisions. However, the circumstances may require that we make decisions.

When Jan and I first seriously discussed whether or not to have a family, we were at Ben Israel Ministries on our first trip to the USA. The past several years had been consumed with working out God's purpose in our lives and we had put off having a family while we pursued this goal. Now that we had accomplished our objective, thoughts of having a family which had taken a back seat became a consideration. As we pondered our decision we wondered what lay ahead for us. What did God want for us in the future? Clearly our trip to the USA confirmed He had a purpose for our lives but what it was we could not say. It seemed to us our coming to the USA was the prelude to a return. We sensed we would be coming back, but could not be sure. Was that God's purpose? If so how would having a family impact that? We needed to make a decision but felt we needed to be more sure about some things.

We prayed about it, and then as we usually do, discussed how we thought God was directing us. "Do you feel God's purpose is we come back to the USA?" I would ask. "Yes I think so, but I am not absolutely certain," Jan would answer. "If we are to come back, how do you think children will affect that?" I would ask. "I don't know," Jan replied. So it went back and forth resolving nothing, getting nowhere. Then one day as we were sitting in the living room of our trailer I suddenly saw what we were doing. We were asking God to reveal the future so we could make our decision. It suddenly came to me that He wasn't going to. As I pondered this thought I came to this conclusion which I blurted out to Jan, "You know, God will not tell us what lies ahead to help us make this decision. I think He is saying it is up to us. We can make the decision freely and it will not affect His purposes for us."

We made the decision to have a family. After discussing it we both found we wanted a family, and on the basis of that desire made the decision to have children. We have four boys. Two were born in New Zealand after we left the States and returned home. The youngest two were born here in the States where we have lived and made our home since 1988. Yes, it was God's will was for us to come back to America as we had intuited. However our decision to have a family did not disqualify us from God's purposes as we feared.

We do not need to know the future to make the right decision. Or, to put it another way; in the absence of any clear guidance from the Lord we are free to make decisions as we see fit with an absolute certainty we will not be lost to the destiny God has for us. The will of God is not some tightrope we walk whereby if we make one false move we fall. On the contrary, it is more like an embankment with walls on either side to keep us on course. Only persistent and willful disobedience takes us away from God. Christians too often are afraid to act, thinking they will miss out on God's perfect will if they make a wrong decision. They make a decision much more complicated than it is as they ponder endless questions that begin 'what if?' They are too afraid of some hidden ulterior motive to ask the one simple question every unbeliever asks when faced with a decision, *"What do you want to do?"* We can make choices in complete confidence God will keep us from harmful choices. Joseph, when he found out Mary was pregnant, was ready to break off the betrothal until an angel came to him and convinced him to proceed with the marriage. Paul the apostle, travelling with Timothy, was trying to go into Bithynia, and the Spirit of Jesus did not permit them (Acts 16:7).

Abraham was a man who set out to walk in the call of God. God had instructed him, *"Go forth from your country, And from your relatives And from your father's house, To the land which I will show you; And I will make you a great nation, And I will bless you, And make your name great; And so you shall be a blessing" (Genesis 12:1.2).* We might expect that at this moment in his life, standing alongside Lot and choosing which direction he would go, he might be carefully weighing all his options and especially taking into account that there was decidedly better pasture in one direction. Yet Abraham was so confidant of the outworking of God's will in his life he left the decision in Lot's hands. He said to Lot, *"Please let there be no strife between you and me, nor between my herdsmen and your herdsmen, for we are brothers. Is not the whole land before you? Please separate from me: if to the left, then I will go to the right; or if to the right, then I will go to the left" (Genesis 13:8.9).* It didn't matter to Abraham which way he went. If Lot went left Abraham would go right, and vice versa. God had promised to bless him and from his seed make a great nation; so far as Abraham was concerned whether he went left or right God would still prosper him.

"In all your ways acknowledge Him, And He will make your paths straight" (Proverbs 3:6). Providing we are in the will of God today we will be in the will of God tomorrow. The will of God is not so much the ability to forecast the future, as what we do today. Regarding the future, we will get there in great shape so long as we make the will of God our priority in the present. God is watching over our life, eager to execute His will. He has a stake in my future as much as I. God is directing the steps of righteous men and women to bring about His purposes in their lives. Being in the will of God is not so much about making the right choices as it is with being a godly person.

Endurance

chapter fifteen

Television did a piece on a young woman selected to represent the United States in basketball at the 2000 Sydney Olympic games. It was all happening so quickly in her life, and beyond her wildest dreams. At first she just thought of basketball as a way to get a scholarship to a university. But women's basketball became a pro sport and before she knew it she was making big money playing professional basketball. And now she was selected to play for the national team at the Olympics. Interviewed on television she said, "I feel like I need to exhale. Pinch me and I will wake up."

When God first showed us we were to go to America I really did not anticipate how long things would take. I'll be honest, there were times when nothing was happening and I would ask myself, "Why am I doing this?" When results do not come quickly the danger is not in turning away from God, but of not maintaining our passion. Those of us in the faith trying to fulfill the purposes of God in our lives definitely find we are in it for the long haul. Endurance is needed, one of the least lauded but essential virtues.

Chapter eleven of Hebrews is known as the faith hall of fame. No doubt a good many of the sermons ever preached on faith would have taken as their text a verse from this chapter. Yet the whole chapter is really a giant parenthesis; we could leave it out altogether without losing the sense of what the author is saying. See for yourself. Try reading the latter half of chapter ten and then going straight to chapter twelve and you will see verse one picks right up where ten left off. At the end of chapter ten the author is talking about the danger of starting out in the faith and then shrinking back. Chapter twelve begins with the statement that because of the example of all the faith heroes just listed, the recipients of his letter ought to run with endurance the race set before them. Chapter eleven is included simply as an illustration to back his argument. The point the writer wants to make in chapter eleven is that all the faith heroes died in the faith. Theirs was a lasting faith. The essence of chapter eleven, if we are to understand it in the context in which it is written, is really about endurance.

We have no idea when we set out in the faith of the concept of endurance. There is a joy and enthusiasm which is good and as it should be, but there is also a naive confidence that does not appreciate that we are in it for the long haul and will need all the resources of concentration and vigor if we are to make it to the end. I remember in high school doing a cross country run in our physical education class. There was much good natured ribbing before the race about beating each other and we started off amidst much chatter and high spirits. As we concluded one lap of the field and headed out the school gates the chatter quieted down. As we made our way across country and up the first incline all talk gave way to heavy breathing. The relief in making it to the top was short lived, for there was yet another hill ahead. Discouraged some began to walk and would be picked up along the route by the teacher following in his car in order to get them back in time for the next class. Others went a little further and then took a short cut back to school. Only those with endurance made it to the finish line.

In the words of the writer of Hebrews the recipients of his letter had become 'sluggish,' and they were 'neglecting their salvation.' They had started out well enough. In the early days some were persecuted for their faith, others had property taken away from them by the authorities and were thrown in prison. The rest of the church eagerly identified with the persecuted and were in turn persecuted themselves. They had all borne it bravely for Christ's sake in the early days. But time had gone by and with it the vitality of their faith. No longer were they encouraging one another in the faith, and some of them were not even assembling together.

The writer warns them their lackadaisical effort puts them at risk. A faith that is brief is not a saving faith - *"For we have become partakers of Christ, if we hold fast the beginning of our assurance firm until the end"* (Hebrews 3:14). A faith that starts out but doesn't hold up does not inherit the promise of God. We need to be careful, as one commentator put it, of the drifting life. Without discipline in spiritual matters we are apt to lose our enthusiasm and wander off course. A neglect of prayer, study in the word, and the regular support and exhortation of others in the faith can be fatal.

By contrast the witnesses in chapter eleven - the men and women in the faith hall of fame - had a strong and vibrant faith that held up until they died. Their endurance was all the more remarkable because they died without receiving the promises. Twice the author makes the point for emphasis; *they never received what they were looking for.* Joseph epitomizes the lasting faith of these heroes when it is said of him he made his brothers swear on his death bed to take his bones up to the land of promise. People who are dying speak about the things that matter most to them. At the end of his life Joseph was concerned most with that which mattered most to him all of his life - the promise God made his grandfather, Abraham, that his descendants would occupy their own land.

'Seeing and welcoming'

What is it about these witnesses in Hebrews chapter eleven that provided their endurance? Let's look at the chapter, particularly verse thirteen as most indicative of endurance: *All these died in faith, without receiving the promises, but having seen them and having welcomed them from a distance, and having confessed that they were strangers and exiles on the earth" (Hebrews 11:13).*

To 'see and welcome' is to embrace the promise of God in a deep and profound way. Mary the mother of Jesus is an example. When the shepherds received the angelic announcement concerning a baby who had been born, they sought the baby and related everything the angels had said concerning the child. It is said those who heard wondered at what they said, *"but Mary treasured up all these things, pondering them in her heart" (Luke 2:19).* The angels revealed a glimpse of the future inspiring in Mary a longing for the reality to which they attested. The phrase, "but having seen them and having welcomed them from a distance," is another way of saying hope. Hope was the anchor of their faith. The promises of God aroused a longing which meant what they had was no longer enough. Hope was the inspiration for their endurance that enabled them to hold out until the end of their lives. So desirable was the promised land that Abraham never considered going back to his homeland once he left, preferring instead the uncertain and insecure life of a sojourner and alien in the land of promise to having a home and place of his own, amongst his own people. So desirable was the promise that Moses and Joseph, both men of privilege and power and wealth in Egypt, preferred to identify themselves with the destiny of the people of Israel, a slave race but the inheritors of God's promise. So desirable was God's promise that all those faith heroes listed in chapter eleven kept after it until they died.

For the joy set before us.

Sometimes the Christian faith is presented in such a way that the pain and discomfort become the objective. This mentality says if there is a road harder to take, that is the one I will take. Let others take their ease and material comforts, as for me I will renounce all worldly pleasures and pursuits. The road to spirituality is through asceticism and self denial. Religion becomes a grim duty. In order to please God I must give up everything and go without. This theology says there is no pleasure or reward in life; just be the man and die to self. In order to get close to God you must give up everything, remove all desire and find that place where you are content with nothing. One preacher I sat under harped constantly on this theme, "Remember it is the cross" and he would repeat several times for emphasis, "it's the cross, it's the cross."

Pain and suffering are not inspirational. The author of Hebrews would have us know that Jesus endured the cross *for the joy set before Him (Hebrews 12:2)*. And although all of those faith heroes listed in chapter eleven did not receive the promises of God, it is clear the promises were the reason they were able to endure. It is a pseudo spirituality that leaves out the idea of reward. If Jesus needed to be motivated by reward, I need not think my faith is likely to endure without motivation of a prize. Those who emphasize suffering as inspirational usually say of Abraham, the father of the faith, that he obeyed God by leaving his country of birth, going out not knowing where he was going. They omit to add that he went out looking for a place God had promised him as an inheritance. Hope started Abraham out in the faith, hope kept him going. If there is nothing to look forward to, endurance is not likely.

Like a lot of rugby-mad New Zealand lads I dreamed of representing my country in a test match. As a youngster I would train for the football season. Out into a wet and cold winter evening I would go and jog the streets for thirty or forty minutes. At the end of my training run was a long twisting hill which seemed to go on and on and on. Three quarters of the way up my chest is pounding, saliva mixes with the rain on my face, my legs feel as if they have weights attached to them. It would be so easy to stop running and walk. I tell myself if I can make it to the top I will be in the national rugby team - an All Black. The image of seeing myself wearing the black jersey and silver fern keeps me going. Up the hill I go, even picking up the pace as I see myself with fourteen other All Blacks getting ready to take the field against our traditional rivals, the South African Springboks. My jog breaks into a run. I am running, I run to the top and sprint the last thirty yards over the brow of the hill and in my mind's eye out onto Eden Park with the crowd roaring.

What I did half way up the hill was to visualize the goal. Anyone who ever had a goal has done the same thing when their will sags. You have to show yourself the goal again if you are to stay on task. The reason the recipients of the letter to the Hebrews were not enduring in the faith was because they were "not holding fast their hope" (Hebrews 10:23). The author reminds the church they had it once, but didn't keep it close. When he says, "Let us hold fast the confession of our hope without wavering," he recognizes the church is drifting away from the faith because they have lost sight of the goal. He is telling them to visualize the goal they had when they started out in the faith. Reminding the church of the hope they had when they started out is an attempt to make them focused and get them back on track. *"You have need of endurance...so you may receive what was promised (Hebrews 10:36).* Promises which he reminds them, were given by God and so cannot fail.

Pain, discipline, deprivation, sacrifice, suffering of one sort or another is the price we pay for the benefit. The question is, how long will we wait for it? How much are we willing to suffer for it? If the objective is really desirable and we really want it, then the potential joy minimizes the discomfort. I always found when I got to the top of the hill I could keep going. I wasn't exhausted even though I pushed myself and ran harder. I got a second wind. So it is in the faith, the anticipation of God's promises makes the load light and enables us to endure. If anyone might have felt justified in letting up on the work God had called him to it was Paul the apostle. He established churches only to hear later they had lapsed in their faith; men he trusted and worked with let him down and in some cases turned against him. Judaizers dogged his footsteps undermining his work every step of the way as he spread the gospel. He was slandered, he was shipwrecked, thrown in jail for his faith, maligned, whipped. All of these trials and tribulations which would have been the undoing of a lesser person Paul dismissed as momentary light affliction because he could see an eternal weight of glory that was his reward: "For momentary, light affliction is producing for us an eternal weight of glory far beyond all comparison…" (2 Corinthians 4:17).

A heavenly city.

There remains something yet to be said concerning the promise of God that inspired and sustained all of these faith heroes. What did they see and welcome? In our key verse we are told their seeing brought forth the confession that they were 'strangers and exiles on the earth.' Something of eternity came into their consideration. Something that looked beyond death. If the promised land by itself were the goal then it would not be true to say they all died without receiving the promise, for some of these faith heroes did indeed possess the land. Earlier on in the letter the author of Hebrews spoke of a rest of God, and in a lengthy argument shows that even though Israel entered the promised land this offer of a rest still stood. While the promise of God did include the physical geographic location we know today as Israel, the promise went further to include a heavenly country; *"But as it is, they desire a better country, that is a heavenly one. Therefore God is not ashamed to be called their God; for He has prepared a city for them"* (Hebrews 11:16).

Because their hope embraced life beyond death it made enduring to the end of their life easier. If the objective of our desire is not grounded in eternity, any delay of hope becomes a stumbling block. When we are not getting results quickly enough and feel like we are up against it all the time, always struggling to no avail, we become discouraged. When the sacrifices and reproaches we have suffered for Christ bring about nothing except further suffering we are apt to ask somewhat discouraged, "What difference does it make anyway?"

The recipients of the letter known as Hebrews looked around and saw nothing had changed as a result of their becoming Christians. Few if any of the citizens of the city in which they lived, had been converted to Christianity. These believers remained a fringe group outside the mainstream of society, ostracized and mistrusted by most people, harassed and persecuted by authorities, the victims of injustice. They hadn't changed the world they lived in, nor had Jesus returned and ushered in His kingdom rule, rewarding their loyalty. For many their earlier single mindedness seems rather pointless. Without an eternal perspective the temptation to take our ease now, in this life, is very real. But if our citizenship is in heaven we won't be tempted to settle down halfway in this life.

Why am I saved? To have a comfortable life here in this world? No, we are saved to prepare for heaven and dwell in the presence of God, forever. God is not the means to an end, He is the end. Here is the ultimate end of our salvation, anything else in this life is a penultimate aim and we should not confuse the two. "My kingdom is not of this world," Jesus told Pilate. "If it was my armies would be fighting for me." Jesus did not place any value on the things to be found in this world. Nor did the faith heroes in chapter eleven who were looking for a heavenly city, and because their hope embraced life beyond death it made enduring to the end of their life easier. In spite of incredible hardship and suffering they were never tempted to take their rest prematurely in this life. They endured, looking for a heavenly country, a city built by God. The blessed hope, the Bible calls this.

The walk of faith is harder than we imagined when we first set out. Few people deliberately turn their back on God. It is far more likely that we stop making the necessary effort. There must be no divided attention, if our faith is to last it must be our best effort and a sustained effort. Only by keeping those hopes that started us out in our faith to the forefront of our consciousness as an incentive will we press forward toward the upward call in Christ Jesus for which we were laid hold of.

Conclusion

Although Moses was one hundred and twenty years old when he died, his eye was not dim, nor his vigor abated (Deuteronomy 34:7).

At the end of his life Moses was just as passionate and dedicated to the task God gave him, as he was when he set out from Egypt all those many years previously. The question is not how well we started out, or what we have done for God in the past, but how are we doing now. Are we witnessing and ministering with the same eagerness and vigor that characterized our early walk in the faith. Do we carry the same hope and anticipation that God will move in our midst? Or have we become weary, disillusioned, perhaps even cynical toward the church.

The call of God is a call to go forward. Moses carried out his charge from God to take the children of Israel to the promised land, and to the end he maintained his enthusiasm and passion for the task God had given him. Now it was time for a new generation to carry on the work of God. As the children of Israel prepared to go into the promised land God exhorted Joshua saying;

"Moses My servant is dead; now therefore arise, cross this Jordan, you and all this people, to the land which I am giving to them, to the sons of Israel. Every place on which the sole of your foot treads, I have given it to you, just as I spoke to Moses.

> *From the wilderness and this Lebanon, even as far as the great river, the river Euphrates, all the land of the Hittites, and as far as the Great Sea toward the setting of the sun, will be your territory"* (Joshua 1:2-4).

Crossing the Jordan was only the beginning. In order to possess the land within the boundaries set forth by God, the Israelites must dispossess the people who occupied those places. God assured Israel they would prevail in any forthcoming conflict; "every place on which the sole of your foot treads, I have given it to you." A careful reading shows the promise is qualified, God's support is conditional upon Israel's willingness to engage the enemy. If the Israelites are to fulfill God's mandate they must set themselves to conquer those cities and peoples who occupy those territories. In the words of scripture they must set their foot on the land. If they are not willing to go up against all the inhabitants and dispossess them, their conquest will be limited. The scope and magnitude of Israel's conquest was up to them.

We too have a destiny, and like Israel, the extent to which we appropriate God's will for our life is up to us. There is a land to be taken for God, it is our heritage. He has marked out its boundaries, in accordance with the spiritual gifting and call He has placed over our life. But we also have an adversary and for us to get our way means Satan suffers loss. No one who is serious about doing God's will can expect they will not be opposed by Satan and their faith tested to it's limits. We have been given a task in establishing God's kingdom, but only if we are bold enough to set our feet upon the land in the first instance and resolute enough to persist in spite of the opposition that stands in our way.

Looking back over my own walk of faith I see how far

the leading of God has brought me. Not just geographically in coming thousands of miles from New Zealand to America, but as a person. I was a nobody in the church. I had no talents or inclinations that leant themselves to ministry. God took a no talent person and has gifted me with the ability to communicate His Word. When I first wrestled with God's calling all those years ago I had no ministry pretensions. I didn't even consider myself a spiritual person. It was others who prayed aloud at church meetings, not me. I was inarticulate and far too reserved to share intimately in public. Those early years were wilderness years. I had a willingness to be used of God, but really no idea what that was, much less how to go about it. I did not fit in anywhere in the church that I could see. When I contemplated how little I had to offer in the way of talent it seemed the height of absurdity to think God could be calling me. More than once I told myself "This is stupid, I am wasting my time." When I was about ready to give up He encouraged me. *"You are a communicator, God is going to use knowledge to flow through you"* was a word of knowledge prophesied over me at a Christian men's retreat. As I stood there head bowed the speaker concluded *"Your hands are important, I see the anointing of God over your hands. Dear Lord bless the fruit of his hands."* And that is exactly how God has used me: to communicate His word, primarily by writing. Which is a marvel for I never had an aptitude or inclination to write growing up. Now I have written a book. God does not see us as we see ourselves, He sees us as the person He intended we should be. He looks at Ken, uncomfortable with public speaking, somewhat ill at ease in large groups, untrained in Bible knowledge and says *"You are a communicator."* There are no 'nobodies' in the church. We all have a talent to be gainfully employed in His service - if it is not evident now, it will be in time.

Living here in the USA I remember the long odds against getting a visa to come and live here. "I believe God is calling me to go back to America. I want to write for God," I remember testifying at a church meeting back home in New Zealand after our first trip to America. Time went by and without any progress toward our goal Satan began to work on me. In the night hours when I was asleep he played with my mind, "God is not telling you to go to America, what an impractical silly idea. That's all it is, you know, just an idea. You went once and had a good time and now you think that is where your future lies. How do you expect to get a visa into America when you have no job skills, no credentials or formal training in ministry? You have no money saved, how will you support yourself when you get there? You want to write, you must be joking. What have you ever written that got published? New Zealand is your home, this is where you belong. You have a good job, good prospects, this is God's will for you, accept it!" Satan is convincing and very plausible. I would wake up persuaded by his logic but with the most cold feeling of futility I have ever known gripping my heart. I would head off for work convinced I should abandon any idea of going to America but thinking at the same time, this is what I want to do. What can I do in place of this that will make my life meaningful?

At work I immersed myself in my job as a commodities broker. My melancholy was soon forgotten in the business of the city markets, dealing with buyers and sellers, arranging shipments of produce and tying up deals. It was not till about mid afternoon after things quieted down, while coming down the back stairs I found myself whistling, thinking about America. I stopped, astonished, remembering the morning and heaviness of spirit. And then I realized what was happening. God was giving me back the hope Satan had stolen that morning. When the reality of our circumstances cause us to despair, only a supernatural work of God can make us hopeful and restore our faith. When Paul wanted to encourage the church in Rome he wrote, *"Now may the God of hope fill you with all joy and peace in believing, that you may abound in hope by the power of the Holy Spirit" (Romans 15:13)*. John the apostle tells us God is love (1 John 4:18), and though scripture does not say so with quite the same succinctness, He is no less hope. To abound in hope when there is no cause to be hopeful is another way of saying being filled with the Holy Spirit. When I look back over my life and the obstacles in my pursuit of God's will I see times when the enemy was too strong for me. I can truly say I overcame not by might, nor by power, but by the Spirit of God. God is committed to our hopes and dreams, because they are His plans for us. He will keep us focused and on track when the enemy is too strong.

Eventually we got our visa and came to America but even here things didn't just fall into place. Nothing opened up in the church that sponsored us. I found myself with a job milking cows facing yet another dead end. All these years and effort, and still no closer to finding my role in the church. It seemed as if it was always eluding me. I felt like a kid who is always looking in the shop window at toys just out of reach. I have got to place myself in the store, I told myself. So the decision was made to pack up and move to Bemidji where we knew some people from our first visit. Once there we planned to start holding meetings in the college. So we packed up all we could in our little vehicle, put the rest in storage and drove 1600 miles across America. Then one day in God's providential arrangement of affairs I was with a friend who stopped off at the local newspaper to do some business. He introduced me to the editor, a friend of his, and when told I was holding meetings at the college he asked if I would like to write a Christian article for the paper. You go after something elusive for so long, then suddenly you turn a corner and there it is before you! I wrote an article, then another, and for five years I wrote a column, "The Living Word", which appeared each week in the newspaper. For the first time since God called me all those years ago in Torbay I felt that I was doing what I was called to do. I felt useful, I had a sense of purpose. I was communicating the knowledge of God to a large audience, many of them people who did not attend church. I was published, I could say "I am a writer." It felt right, it felt good. I always felt a sense of accomplishment on a Friday when I met my deadline and took my disc containing the week's column downtown to the newspaper office. Sometimes upon meeting people they would tell me they read my column and how much something I said had meant to them. I had found my niche. Isn't this the journey we all make in life, to find ourselves, and in the process discover our destiny?

There are some twists in the road, and there are times you just want to give up in the area of your mind. But if we hang in there, not drawing back, eventually a way will open up. The characteristic that marks out those men and women who are fulfilling their destiny is that they are over-comers. They overcome the adversities in their life that thwart those less resolute. They overcome by God's enabling power, who is watching over them, eager and desirous to work out His will in their life. When you succeed words cannot express the heart felt joy and soul peace in being in the center of God's will. And it is only the beginning. It is a broad place He has brought us. As far as we have come, there is a potential for ministry that we may barely have stepped into.

"He sent from on high, He took me; He drew me out of many waters.

He delivered me from my strong enemy, And from those who hated me, for they were too mighty for me.

They confronted me in the day of my calamity, But the LORD was my stay.

He brought me forth also into a broad place; He rescued me, because He delighted in me" (Psalm 18:16-19).